ELEANOR ROOSEVELT

A Life of Discovery

ELEANOR ROOSEVELT

A Life of Discovery

RUSSELL FREEDMAN

CLARION BOOKS | NEW YORK

Clarion Books
a Houghton Mifflin Company imprint
215 Park Avenue South, New York, NY 10003
Text copyright © 1993 by Russell Freedman

FRONTISPIECE: Mrs. Roosevelt playfully raps for order as she
prepares to introduce her husband at the National Education
Association convention in New York, June 30, 1938.

Library of Congress Cataloging-in-Publication Data
Freedman, Russell.
Eleanor Roosevelt : a life of discovery / by Russell Freedman.
p.   cm.
Includes bibliographical references and index.
Summary: A photobiography of the first wife of a president to have
a public life and career of her own.
ISBN 0-89919-862-7
1. Roosevelt, Eleanor, 1884–1962—Juvenile literature.
2. Presidents—United States—Wives—Biography—Juvenile literature.
[1. Roosevelt, Eleanor, 1884–1962.   2. First ladies.]   I. Title.
E807.1.R48F74   1993
[B]   973.917′092—dc20   92-25024
                                                CIP
                                                AC

HOR   10 9 8 7 6 5 4 3

For Isabella Halsted

Contents

You gain strength, courage and confidence
by every experience in which you really
stop to look fear in the face. . . .
You must do the thing you think
you cannot do.

ELEANOR ROOSEVELT

The most influential woman of her time.

ONE

First Lady

Eleanor Roosevelt never wanted to be a president's wife. When her husband Franklin won his campaign for the presidency in 1932, she felt deeply troubled. She dreaded the prospect of living in the White House.

Proud of her accomplishments as a teacher, a writer, and a political power in her own right, she feared that she would have to give up her hard-won independence in Washington. As First Lady, she would have no life of her own. Like other presidential wives before her, she would be assigned the traditional role of official White House hostess, with little to do but greet guests at receptions and preside over formal state dinners.

"From the personal standpoint, I did not want my husband to be president," she later confessed. "It was pure selfishness on my part, and I never mentioned my feelings on the subject to him."

Mrs. Roosevelt did her duty. During her years in the White House, the executive mansion bustled with visitors at teas, receptions, and dinners. At the same time, however, she cast her fears aside and seized the opportunity to transform the role of America's First Lady. Encouraged by her friends, she became the first wife of a president to have a public life and career.

Americans had never seen a First Lady like her. She was the first to open the White House door to reporters and hold on-the-record press conferences, the first to drive her own car, to travel by plane, and to make many official trips by herself. "My missus goes where she wants to!" the president boasted.

She was the first president's wife to earn her own money by writing, lecturing, and broadcasting. Her earnings usually topped the president's salary. She gave most of the money to charity.

When she insisted on her right to take drives by herself, without a chauffeur or a police escort, the Secret Service, worried about her safety, gave her a pistol and begged her to carry it with her. "I [took] it and learned how to use it," she told readers of her popular newspaper column. "I do not mean by this that I am an expert shot. I only wish I were. . . . My opportunities for shooting have been far and few between, but if the necessity arose, I do know how to use a pistol."

She had come a long way since her days as an obedient society matron, and, before then, a timid child who was "always afraid of something." By her own account, she had been an "ugly duckling" whose mother told her, "You have no looks, so see to it that you have manners." Before she was

MRS. ROOSEVELT CARRIES A PISTOL!

'Packs' a Weapon on Lone Auto Journeys---And Knows How to Use It

NEW ORLEANS, March 6 (U.P.).—Mrs. Eleanor Roosevelt modestly revealed today that she is somewhat of a marksman with a pistol.

She was trained, she said, by New York State prison guards as a matter of protection when she drives about the country alone.

In a press conference here preceding the first of a series of lectures on a six-State tour, the President's wife casually told of her adeptness with a gun. She said:

"Only when I travel by automobile—that is, when I drive alone, have I any protection. And then I carry a pistol."

"Can you use a pistol?" asked astonished reporters. She replied: "Oh, yes, I was trained by the prison guards of New York and I'm a fairly good shot."

At her lecture, Mrs. Roosevelt reemphasized that she had no desire to become President of the United States. The time is not yet ripe, she said, for women in that field.

"Not that many of them are not worthy, but at this time no woman can obtain and hold the support necessary for election."

Mrs. Roosevelt was to speak in Baton Rouge tonight.

MRS. FRANKLIN D. ROOSEVELT AT WHEEL OF HER AUTOMOBILE
First Lady was Starting for a Drive Through Rock Creek Park.

When the First Lady insisted on driving her own car, the Secret Service begged her to carry a pistol.

ten, both of her unhappy parents were dead. She grew up in a time and place where a woman's life was ruled by her husband's interests and needs, and dominated by the domestic duties of a wife and mother. "It was not until I reached middle age," she wrote, "that I had the courage to develop interests of my own, outside of my duties to my family."

Eleanor Roosevelt lived in the White House during the Great Depression and the Second World War. In her endless travels through America, she served as a fact-finder and trouble-shooter for her husband and an impassioned publicist for her own views about social justice and world peace. She wanted people to feel that their government cared about them. After Franklin Roosevelt's death, she became a major force at the United Nations, where her efforts on behalf of human rights earned her the title, First Lady of the World.

People meeting her for the first time often were startled by how "unjustly" the camera treated her. Photographs had not prepared them for her warmth and dignity and poise. An unusually tall woman, she moved with the grace of an athlete, and when she walked into a room, the air seemed charged with her vibrancy. "No one seeing her could fail to be moved," said her friend Martha Gellhorn. "She gave off light, I cannot explain it better."

For thirty years, from the time she entered the White House until her death in 1962, Eleanor Roosevelt was the most famous and at times the most influential woman in the world. And yet those who knew her best were most impressed by her simplicity, by her total lack of self-importance.

"About the only value the story of my life may have," she wrote, "is to show that one can, even without any particular gifts, overcome obstacles that seem insurmountable if one is willing to face the fact that they must be overcome; that, in spite of timidity and fear, in spite of a lack of special talents, one can find a way to live widely and fully."

Eleanor at age three.

TWO

Poor Little Rich Girl

*"Looking back it strikes me that my childhood and my
early youth were one long battle against fear."*

Eleanor Roosevelt stood in the doorway, her finger in her mouth, too
timid to enter the room. Her mother was sitting in an armchair by the
fireplace, sipping tea and chatting with a friend.

At long last her mother glanced up and saw Eleanor standing there.
"Come in, Granny," she sighed. Turning to her guest, Mrs. Roosevelt
confided, "She is such a funny child, so old-fashioned that we always call
her 'Granny.' "

Eleanor wanted to sink through the floor in shame. Forty years later she
could still see the look in her mother's eyes and hear the tone of her voice
as she said, "Come in, Granny."

"She often called me that," Eleanor recalled, "for I was a solemn child,
without beauty and painfully shy."

Eleanor knew that she was plain at best, "a blue-eyed rather ugly little
girl" who bit her fingernails and seldom smiled. Her mother, Anna, was
"one of the most beautiful women I have ever seen." Growing up, Eleanor
felt that she must have been a disappointment to Anna.

"My mother was troubled by my lack of beauty," she wrote in her
autobiography. "I knew it as a child senses these things. She tried hard to
bring me up well so that my manners would compensate for my looks, but

5

her efforts only made me more keenly conscious of my shortcomings."

Her father, Elliott, was a handsome man-about-town, a dashing sportsman who had hunted tigers and elephants in India. Eleanor adored her father. One of her earliest memories was of being allowed to dress up and dance for him and his friends. They laughed and applauded as she whirled and pirouetted before them in the dining room. Then her father would sweep her up and hold her high in the air and kiss her. "With my father I was perfectly happy," she wrote. "He was the center of my world and all around him loved him."

Eleanor's parents were socialites, at home in the drawing rooms and ballrooms of New York's high society. Anna Hall had been a glamorous debutante, admired for her stunning beauty and grace. Elliott belonged to the exclusive Meadow Brook Country Club. His life revolved around polo, fox-hunting, and horse shows. When he was courting Anna, he gave her a spectacular tiger-claw necklace he had brought back from India. He had shot the tiger himself.

Their marriage in 1883 had united two old and prominent families. The first Roosevelts had arrived in the New World during the 1640s, when New Amsterdam (later to be called New York) was a tiny Dutch settlement at the foot of Manhattan Island. Anna's ancestors had signed the Declaration of Independence and administered the oath of office to President George Washington.

Their first child, Anna Eleanor Roosevelt, was born under a full moon on October 11, 1884. Though the infant girl was "a more wrinkled and less attractive baby than average," Elliott called her "a miracle from heaven." His older brother Theodore—later to be the president of the United States—was baby Eleanor's delighted godfather.

Eleanor was welcomed into a golden world of privilege and wealth. Her parents lived in style and comfort on their ample inheritances. They owned a townhouse staffed with servants on a fashionable Manhattan street. Anna had her own horse and carriage. She ordered her dresses from London and Paris. Elliott had four fine polo ponies stabled at his Long Island country club. His gaiety and high spirits, and Anna's luminous grace, made them one of the most sought-after couples on the New York social scene.

Eleanor's father and mother were wealthy New York socialites. They recorded her birth in the Roosevelt family Bible.

A French nurse looked after Eleanor. The little girl spent so much time with her nurse that she spoke French before she spoke English.

Elliott Roosevelt was gifted with a warm and generous nature that charmed nearly everyone. "He is such a tender, sympathetic, manly man," said his sister. But he was also a deeply troubled young man. Nervous and moody, he seemed unable to settle down. He would go off on drinking sprees with his friends and come home reeking of liquor.

Eleanor was not yet five when her father shattered his ankle while practicing somersaults for a society circus. Improperly set, the ankle had to be rebroken and set again. Night after night that summer, Elliott's cries of pain echoed through the house. Eleanor, who wept when a playmate was injured, would dissolve in tears as she listened to her father's suffering. To numb his pain, Elliott drank more heavily and began to take morphine and laudanum—two powerful pain-killing drugs that doctors prescribed freely at that time.

Anna tried desperately to steady her young husband. She begged him to break his dependence on alcohol and drugs. After the birth of their second child, Elliott, Jr., in 1889, Elliott left his family and traveled south in search of a cure. "I do nothing but think of you and pray you will come back," Anna wrote to him. "Dearest, Throw your horrid cocktails away and don't touch anything hard. . . . Remember that your little wife and children love you so tenderly and will try to help you in every possible way they can to conquer in the hard hard fight."

When Elliott returned, he vowed to do better. But he was not "cured." He rattled about the house on sleepless nights, struggled with bouts of depression, and continued to drink.

Determined to keep her family together, Anna persuaded Elliott to take them on a leisurely tour of European health resorts. For several months the family wandered through Germany, Austria, Italy, and France. Anna watched anxiously over her husband. For a time, he behaved himself.

Six-year-old Eleanor was now able to spend every single day with her father. In Venice, he acted as a gondolier, taking his daughter out on the canals and, as Eleanor recalled, "singing with the other boatmen, to my intense joy. I loved his voice and, above all, I loved the way he treated me. . . . I never doubted that I stood first in his heart."

Elliott Roosevelt with his children: Elliott, Jr., baby Hall on his father's lap, and Eleanor. Elliott, Jr., died of diphtheria a few months after this photo was taken.

Eleanor's greatest wish was to please her father. She dreaded his disapproval. The one thing that annoyed Elliott was his daughter's fearfulness. "I was not only timid," Eleanor recalled, "I was afraid. Afraid of almost everything, I think: of mice, of the dark, of imaginary dangers. . . ." She tried to hide her fears from her father.

In the mountains of Italy one day, Eleanor was riding a donkey when they came to a steep downhill slope. She turned pale with fright and hung back. Her father looked down at her from his horse and asked if she wanted to turn back. "You are not afraid are you?" he said. For the rest of her life she remembered the tone of disapproval in his voice.

A third child, Hall, was born in Paris in June 1891. By then, Elliott was drinking again. He disappeared into the city for days at a time, moaned that he was losing his mind, and talked openly of suicide. That summer,

At age eight, Eleanor poses with Hall for a Christmas portrait.

he entered a French sanitarium. Anna gathered the children and sailed back to New York without him.

At this point, Elliott's brother, Theodore, stepped in to take charge of the family's affairs. Theodore hurried to Paris and confronted his unhappy brother. He demanded that Elliott spend two full years of probation on his own, away from Anna and the children. He would not be allowed to return to his family until he proved that he had rehabilitated himself.

Elliott agreed to go into exile. He settled in the small town of Abingdon, Virginia, where he would manage a brother-in-law's sprawling woodlands and coal mines.

In New York, Anna tried to raise her children and resume her life alone. She had not wanted to give up her husband, and she missed him terribly, but she felt humiliated by his behavior. She told Elliott's sister that she was "desperately lonely and wildly furious with the world at large. . . . I hate everything and everyone so and am most of the time so miserable. . . ."

Eleanor was seven years old now. She did not understand why her father was not with them, or why her mother seemed so distant and preoccupied. No one in the family would explain what had happened. Had her mother sent her father away?

Lying in bed at night, she would try to listen to the hushed voices of her mother and aunts downstairs as they murmured anxiously about Elliott. "I acquired a strange and garbled view of the troubles around me," she wrote. "Something was wrong with my father and from my point of view nothing could be wrong with him."

Anna did her best to reassure her children. Every evening she would gather them around her for "mother's hour," when she would read to them and play with them. "My little brother Ellie adored her, and was so good he never had to be reproved," Eleanor recalled. The baby Hall was content to sit quietly on his mother's lap. Eleanor would sit on a footstool, apart from the others. "I felt a curious barrier between myself and these three," she wrote.

Anna tried to give her daughter special attention. Eleanor slept in her mother's bedroom. She remembered "the thrill of watching her dress to go out in the evenings. She looked so beautiful I was grateful to be allowed to touch her dress or her jewels or anything that was part of the vision which I admired. . . ."

To make up for Eleanor's neglected education, Anna hired a private tutor. She turned the upper floor of their house into a schoolroom and invited the daughters of several friends to share Eleanor's lessons. "My mother made a great effort," Eleanor wrote later. And yet she felt that no matter what she did, she could never fully earn her mother's approval.

That winter Anna suffered from agonizing headaches and backaches and complained that her eyes were failing. She would draw the curtains and spend hours in bed until the pains subsided. Eleanor would sit silently with her in the dark and gently stroke her mother's head. "Perhaps even as a child there was something soothing in my touch, for she was willing to let me sit there for hours on end," Eleanor wrote. "The feeling that I was useful was perhaps the greatest joy I experienced."

Just before Eleanor's eighth birthday, her mother entered the hospital to have surgery for some unknown illness. Elliott wanted to travel north to be with his wife, but he was asked to stay away. Anna did not want him to come. He never saw her again. After her operation she contracted diphtheria, and, at the age of twenty-nine, Anna Roosevelt died. When Elliott received the news in Virginia, he hurriedly packed a bag and flagged the night train to New York.

Eleanor had been sent to stay with relatives. "I can remember standing by a window when Cousin Susie told me that my mother was dead," she wrote. "Death meant nothing to me, and one fact wiped out everything else. My father was back and I would see him soon."

She did not see him right away. In her will, Anna had asked that her children be raised by her own mother, Mary Hall. And so Eleanor and her brothers were sent to live with Grandmother Hall in her gloomy Manhattan brownstone. After they were settled, Elliott came to visit. Eleanor remembered going downstairs to the dim, high-ceilinged library, where her father was sitting in a big chair:

"He was dressed all in black, looking very sad. He held out his arms and gathered me to him. In a little while he began to talk, to explain to me that my mother was gone, that she had been all the world to him, and now he had only my brothers and myself, that my brothers were very young and that he and I must keep close together. Someday I would make a home for him again. . . .

"There started that day a feeling which never left me, that he and I were very close and someday would have a life of our own together. He told me to write to him often, to be a good girl, not to give any trouble, to study hard, to grow up into a woman he could be proud of, and he would come to see me whenever it was possible."

Elliott went back to Virginia. Eleanor wrote to him regularly. She cherished the long, affectionate letters she received in return.

Exiled to Virginia, Eleanor's father raised prize terriers.

> *July 10th 1894*
>
> *Dear Father*
> *I hope you are not Iamnow in Bar-Harbor and am having a lovely time yesterday I went to the Indian encampn to see some pretty things I have to find out the paths all alone I walked up to the top of Nebo mountain this morning and I walk three hours every afternoon Brudie walks from 4 to 5 miles every day. Please write to me soon. We eat our meals at the hotel and the names of the things we get to eat ar to funny Washington pie an and blanket of Veal are mild to some other things we get. I have lessons every day with Grandma. With a great deal of love Ia your little daughter. Nell.*

One of Eleanor's last letters to her father, signed "your little daughter, Nell," Elliott's pet name for her.

That spring, she was sent to stay with relatives when both of her brothers came down with scarlet fever. Baby Hall recovered, but three-year-old Ellie developed diphtheria and died of the same disease that had killed his mother. Eleanor tried to comfort her father. "We must rember [sic] Ellie is going to be safe in heaven and to be with Mother," she wrote to him.

Back at Grandmother Hall's house, Eleanor looked forward to her father's letters and his irregular visits. Meanwhile, she lived "in a dreamworld in which I was the heroine and my father the hero. Into this world I withdrew as soon as I went to bed and as soon as I woke up in the morning and all the time I was walking or when anyone bored me."

Elliott showered his daughter with gifts—a kitten, a fox terrier puppy "because he knew I would love to have something to care for and call my own," a pony to ride at her grandmother's country house. When the doorbell rang and Eleanor heard her father's voice, she would race from her room, slide down two flights of bannisters, and fly into his arms. They took long walks together and happy carriage rides through Central Park. When Elliott mentioned that he liked Longfellow's *The Song of Hiawatha*, Eleanor memorized part of the long epic poem so she could recite it to him on his next visit.

Elliott wasn't always reliable. Sometimes he failed to show up when he had promised to visit. And when he did come to New York, things did not always go well. Once, when Eleanor went walking with her father and three of his prize terriers, he stopped at the Knickerbocker Club, handed his daughter the leashes, and told her to wait with the doorman while he went in for a drink. Eleanor waited. Six hours later, as she remembered it, she watched as her father was carried senseless out of the club and helped into a passing cab.

After that, Grandmother Hall discouraged even brief visits from Elliott. She would call him "the dearest man I ever knew, so gentle, and kind-hearted." But now that he was drinking heavily again, she feared his visits and wanted to shield the children from him.

Elliott began to slip in and out of the city without telling anyone. A note to Grandmother Hall said, "I have a desolate feeling that I cannot overcome—but I do not care to see anyone." In the summer of 1894, he lapsed into a coma after a drunken fall and died with none of his family around him.

Eleanor was not yet ten. Her aunts broke the news to her, and that night she cried herself to sleep: "While I wept long and went to bed still weeping I finally went to sleep and began the next day living in my dreamworld as usual. . . . From that time on I knew in my mind that my father was dead, and yet I lived with him more closely, probably, than I had when he was alive."

Orphans now, Eleanor and her brother, Hall, continued to live with their grandmother and her own unruly brood of eccentric sons and daughters. Grandmother Hall spent most of the day alone in her room. She came downstairs only to greet an infrequent visitor, and to conduct morning and evening prayer services for the family and household servants. Though her children were grown, four of them still lived at home—two beautiful but temperamental daughters, Aunts Pussie and Maude, and two high-spirited playboy sons, Uncles Vallie and Eddie.

For years, Mary Hall had tried to cope with the tempestuous love affairs of her daughters and the wild escapades of her sons. By the time Eleanor and Hall arrived in the household, their grandmother seemed exhausted.

She had taken the orphans in with kindness and loving concern, but now that they were under her care, she was determined that they should have the strict discipline her own children had lacked. "We were brought up on the principle that 'no' was easier to say than 'yes,' " Eleanor recalled.

Mrs. Hall was convinced that her granddaughter suffered from curvature of the spine. For nearly a year, Eleanor had to wear a steel brace "which was vastly uncomfortable and prevented my bending over." Later, like her mother and aunts before her, she was made to practice erect ladylike posture by walking endlessly back and forth with a stick behind her shoulders, hooked at her elbows.

Her younger cousin Corinne Robinson lived nearby. Though Corinne was fond of Eleanor, she would visit only when her mother insisted. "I never wanted to go," she remembered. "The grim atmosphere of that house. There was no place to play games, unbroken gloom everywhere. We ate our suppers in silence. . . . The general attitude was, 'don't do this.' "

Eleanor continued to attend classes taught by a private tutor, held now at the townhouse of a classmate. A conscientious student, she mastered arithmetic with difficulty, loved poetry, and wrote sad stories about lonely children who yearned for love.

At home she took piano lessons, and while she practiced faithfully, "no one ever trained my ear!" she complained. However, her aunt Pussie was a fine pianist. "She played with great feeling," Eleanor wrote. "I would lie on the sofa and listen to her for hours." From Pussie she gained a lasting "emotional appreciation of music."

Eleanor also attended a fashionable dance school, where the children of socially prominent families were initiated into the mysteries of the waltz, the two-step, and the polka. The instructor, Mr. Dodsworth, was "dapper and very slim and very correct and kept us in order with what looked like a pair of castanets." Mrs. Dodsworth, at the piano, always wore an evening dress.

Those classes were an agony for Eleanor. She was skinny and tall for her age, with prominent teeth and a small chin. And her grandmother's choice of clothes for her made it worse. Mary Hall insisted that Eleanor

"I was fond of horses but not of long stockings and high shoes." Eleanor was photographed with her pony at Oak Terrace, her grandmother's country house.

*With her bicycle at
Oak Terrace.*

*A page from a journal
that Eleanor kept when
she was fourteen.*

Nov. 18. I have a headache journal to-night & I am feeling cross. Poor Auntie Pussie she is so worried I am going to try & see if I can do something for her to-night. Have studied hard this lessons but I can't think of a composition I suppose I can think to-morrow morning. Am not going to tell Mr — unless something happens. Have tried to be good & sweet & quiet but have not succeeded. Oh my. Alice did not come, I never will see her I am afraid I wish I could but I don't dare ask if she is coming to lunch. I do hope I will see her. Goodnight journal.

wear long black stockings, old-fashioned, high-button shoes, and "dresses that were above my knees, when most of the girls my size had them halfway down their legs." Eleanor knew that the other girls laughed at her behind her back.

Her happiest times were spent at Oak Terrace, Grandmother Hall's big secluded country house atop a high bluff overlooking the Hudson River. Eleanor loved the countryside around Oak Terrace. On summer mornings she would get up before dawn and walk with Aunt Pussie through misty woods down to the river. They would climb into a small boat, row five miles to the town of Tivoli, pick up the mail, then row back in time for breakfast.

One summer Uncle Vallie taught her to jump her pony. Now and then there were carefree picnics and carriage rides with her aunts and uncles. But often, Eleanor's only companion at Oak Terrace was her brother, who was nearly seven years younger. She spent most of the summer lost in books and in her private dreamworld.

For years she dreamed of becoming a singer, so she could win attention and admiration. "I would have given anything to be a singer," she wrote. "Attention and admiration were the things . . . I wanted, because I was made to feel so conscious of the fact that nothing about me would attract attention or would bring me admiration."

The year Eleanor turned fourteen she was allowed to attend Aunt Corinne's annual Christmas Party. She wasn't used to being with boys her own age, and the weekend event caused her "more pain than pleasure," she recalled. "The others all knew each other and saw each other often. They were all much better at winter sports."

The highlight of the weekend was a formal dance. As usual, Eleanor was dressed like a little girl in a short dress with blue bows on each shoulder and the hem above her knees. The other girls came dressed as sophisticated young ladies. "I knew, of course, that I was different from all the other girls and if I had not known they were frank in telling me so!" she wrote.

Mortified, Eleanor stood miserably against a wall that evening, trying to stretch her dress down over her knees as she watched her sparkling cousin Alice in a long gown dance with another cousin, sixteen-year-old Franklin

"I was tall, very thin, and very shy."

Delano Roosevelt. When the dance ended, Alice whispered in Franklin's ear. He turned his head, glanced at Eleanor, then sauntered over and asked her for the next dance. She never forgot her gratitude.

"Poor little soul, she is very plain," wrote her aunt Edith. "Her mouth and teeth seem to have no future. But the ugly duckling may turn out to be a swan."

Eleanor at age fifteen.

THREE

Mademoiselle Souvestre

"I felt that I was starting a new life, free from all my former sins and traditions . . . this was the first time in my life that all my fears left me. If I lived up to the rules and told the truth, there was nothing to fear."

Eleanor's mother had wanted to send her to Europe for part of her education. When she was fifteen, her grandmother honored that wish by enrolling her in Allenswood, an exclusive girls' finishing school on the outskirts of London.

Grandmother Hall wrote to the school's headmistress, Marie Souvestre, telling her about Eleanor's troubled childhood. She was a good girl, Mary Hall reported, but sadly unattractive and full of fears. Sometimes she was afraid to tell the truth. And she suffered from headaches and sleeplessness.

Eleanor arrived at Allenswood in September 1899. Accompanied by an aunt, she was carrying all of her father's letters in a bundle tied with a ribbon. Mademoiselle Souvestre greeted her warmly. A magnetic French woman about seventy, she had keen gray eyes and silvery hair drawn back in the manner of a Greek statue. "Her eyes looked through you," wrote Eleanor, "and she always knew more than she was told."

Most of the thirty-five students at Allenswood were British, but they were required to speak French at all times. If a girl used an English word by mistake, she had to report herself at the end of the day. This was no hardship for Eleanor. At her first meal, a classmate remembered, "when we hardly dared open our mouths, she sat opposite Mlle. Souvestre chatting away in French . . . we admired her courage."

The students lived in a drafty brick building where "one had positively to sit on the radiator to feel any warmth." All the girls wore uniforms—straw hats, white ruffled blouses with striped school neckties, and dark ankle-length skirts. Each girl was allowed just three ten-minute baths a week. After breakfast, they all went for a brisk walk on the school common, no matter how cold the weather. While they were in class, their rooms were inspected. If a closet or bureau drawer wasn't neat enough, the owner would find its contents dumped on her bed when she returned to her room.

The rules were strict, but the atmosphere at Allenswood was charged with excitement. An inspired teacher, Mademoiselle Souvestre challenged her students to open their minds and imaginations and think for themselves. Listening to her conversation in the classroom or at the dinner table "was an education in itself," said a former student. "Her brilliant speech darted here and there with the agility and grace of a hummingbird. . . . Every subject, however dull it had seemed in the hands of others, became animated in hers."

Mademoiselle Souvestre taught history and literature in her library, a spacious room lined with books and filled with flowers. Eleanor enjoyed these classes more than any others. The students sat on little chairs on either side of the fireplace, watching the compact figure of their headmistress as she strode back and forth, jabbing at a wall map with a long wooden pointer, hurling questions, creating vivid word pictures that made the great events of the past come alive. If a girl handed in an essay that was not carefully thought through, or that simply parroted Souvestre's own ideas, the headmistress thought nothing of tearing it up in front of the class and letting the pieces flutter to the floor.

In the evenings, Marie Souvestre might invite a few girls to her study. She had a great talent for reading poems and stories aloud, always in French. She would often discuss politics and public affairs, subjects that were never mentioned among Grandmother Hall's closed circle of friends. Souvestre had a special sympathy for unpopular causes. She always championed the underdog. "I found this an exhilarating way to spend an evening," Eleanor wrote. "Mlle. Souvestre shocked me into thinking, and that on the whole was very beneficial."

The student body at Allenswood.

Eleanor (back row, third from right) with her classmates.

Souvestre recognized in Eleanor special qualities of mind and spirit that her grandmother's letter hadn't mentioned. Before long, she assigned Eleanor a place of honor across from the headmistress at the dining table. The girl who occupied this place would watch for Souvestre's nod at the end of a meal, then give the signal, by rising, for the rest of the girls to rise and leave the dining room.

By the time the Christmas holidays came around, Eleanor felt at home at Allenswood. She slept soundly. Her headaches vanished. She was never ill, even for a day. She stopped biting her nails. Everything about the school seemed to agree with her.

As her fears faded, her personality shone forth. For the first time in her life, she made friends easily. She even did well at sports and earned a place on the first hockey team, "one of the proudest moments of my life."

"She is full of sympathy for all those who live with her and shows an intelligent interest in everything she comes in contact with," Mademoiselle Souvestre reported to Grandmother Hall. Eleanor responded to all this attention by living up to Souvestre's expectations.

During school holidays, the headmistress invited Eleanor to join her on trips to France and Italy. "This was one of the most momentous things that happened in my education," Eleanor remembered. Until then, she had always traveled with relatives or with a chaperone who took care of everything. Mademoiselle Souvestre gave her the responsibilities of a full-fledged traveling companion. It was Eleanor's job to check train schedules and purchase tickets, and to do all the packing and unpacking for both of them.

"Traveling with Mlle. Souvestre was a revelation," she wrote. "She did all the things that in a vague way you had always felt you wanted to do." They stayed in small hotels that saw few foreigners, ate the local food, went off the beaten track, and changed plans on the spur of the moment. One evening in Italy, Souvestre suddenly decided to grab their bags and get off a train in the middle of their journey, so they could walk on a beach and see the Mediterranean in the moonlight. "Never again would I be the rigid little person I had been before," wrote Eleanor.

While everyone knew that she was Mademoiselle Souvestre's "supreme

Headmistress Marie Souvestre. "She shocked me into thinking," wrote Eleanor.

favorite," she was also popular with her other teachers and her school-mates. During her last year at Allenswood, her cousin Corinne entered the school. Corrine was the girl who had once felt sorry for Eleanor. Now she found that her cousin was a different person. "When I arrived she was 'everything' at the school," Corinne wrote. "She was beloved by everybody."

The younger girls especially looked up to her. On Saturdays, when they were allowed to go into town and make small purchases, they would always return with gifts for Eleanor. "Eleanor's room every Saturday would be full of flowers because she was so admired," Corinne reported.

Eleanor would later call her three years at Allenswood "the happiest of my life." She had come to the school feeling "lost and very lonely"—a shy, awkward girl starved for love and approval. She left in triumph,

Traveling on the Continent during a school holiday, Eleanor shows off a new suit and hat.

having earned the affection and esteem of her classmates, her teachers, and her headmistress.

She wanted to stay on for a fourth year, but Grandmother Hall had summoned her back to America to make her formal debut in New York society. "To my grandmother," she wrote, "the age of eighteen was the time when you 'came out,' and not to 'come out' was unthinkable."

Marie Souvestre worried about her young friend. In New York, Souvestre feared, Eleanor would be swept up in the social whirl of debutante dances and parties, and her special gifts of sympathy and intelligence would be wasted. And yet the headmistress also worried that Eleanor was perhaps too serious for her own good. It seemed that she could never be as lighthearted or as carefree as other young people. After telling Corinne about Eleanor's many virtues, Mademoiselle Souvestre would throw up her hands and add, *"mais elle n'est pas gaie"*—"but she is not joyful."

Eleanor believed that her encounter with Marie Souvestre's "liberal mind and strong personality" had changed her life. "Mlle. Souvestre had become one of the people whom I cared most for in the world," she wrote, "and the thought of the long separation seemed hard to bear."

And Souvestre in turn thought the world of Eleanor. She told Grandmother Hall that Eleanor had "the warmest heart that I have ever encountered." When Eleanor returned to New York that summer, the headmistress wrote: "I miss you every day of my life."

Back home, Eleanor had to face family troubles and the terrors of her social debut. She spent a miserable summer at her grandmother's country house. Her uncle Vallie, "who had been so kind to me when I was a child, had been slipping rapidly into the habits of the habitual drinker."

Vallie's drinking was out of control. He rampaged through the house and crouched at an upstairs window with a shotgun, firing wildly at anything in sight. Eleanor and her brother Hall hugged the trunks of the big shade trees when they dared to cross the lawn. Uncle Eddie was married now, but he sometimes came home to join his brother in a drunken spree. Grandmother Hall seemed helpless to restrain her sons.

Mortified, she had cut herself off from contact with the neighbors. "That first summer was not good preparation for being a gay and joyous debutante," wrote Eleanor.

That fall, Hall went to boarding school and Eleanor returned to her grandmother's townhouse in Manhattan, where she had to cope with the stormy emotional life of her aunt Pussie. Fourteen years Eleanor's senior, Pussie was still falling in and out of love. When one of her romances went sour, she would lock herself in her room and sulk for days at a time.

On weekends, Vallie and Eddie might show up arm in arm, ready to carouse again. Eleanor was so frightened by their behavior that she installed triple locks on the inside of her bedroom door. One weekend when she was visiting her aunt Corinne, she burst into tears and sobbed, "Auntie, I have no real home!"

Meanwhile, she had to prepare for her debut. She would be eighteen in October. In December, she would "come out" with other socially prominent girls at the lavish Assembly Ball at the Waldorf-Astoria Hotel.

A debut was considered the ultimate test of a young lady's social talents. As the time approached, Eleanor's fears and anxieties surfaced again. In their own time, her mother, her grandmother, and her aunts had been among the most beautiful debutantes in New York. They had won the admiration of many beaux. Eleanor felt that she could never measure up to what a Roosevelt or Hall woman was expected to be.

On the evening of the Assembly Ball, she was fashionably turned out in a gown Aunt Tissie had ordered from Paris. Her hair was artfully arranged in the latest style. But she was convinced that she was too tall, too serious, and too plain, and that she did not dance well. "I imagine I was well dressed," she wrote, "but there was absolutely nothing about me to attract anybody's attention."

The Assembly Ball was a frightening event for "ninety-nine percent of us," according to one debutante. All the girls were anxious about their looks, their gowns, and above all, how many young men would ask them to dance. For Eleanor, the ball was truly an ordeal. She had lost touch with most of the girls she had known before going to England, and she knew only two eligible men, both much older than she.

A New York society ball.

*Eleanor at eighteen:
her "coming out" photo.*

"I do not think I quite realized beforehand what utter agony it was going to be or I would never have had the courage to go," she wrote. "Bob Ferguson [a Roosevelt family friend] introduced a number of his friends but by no stretch of the imagination could I fool myself into thinking I was a popular debutante!

"I went home early, thankful to get away. . . . I knew I was the first girl in my mother's family who was not a belle and, though I never acknowledged it to any of them at that time, I was deeply ashamed."

Actually, Eleanor was more successful as a debutante than she admitted to herself. That winter she was invited to many of the exclusive dinners, dances, and theater parties that signified social success. Usually she was escorted by Bob Ferguson, "who lived a pleasant bachelor existence in New York and had many friends." And yet, compared to her glamorous aunts and beautiful mother, she felt inadequate.

"That first winter, when my sole object in life was society, nearly brought me to a state of nervous collapse," she confessed. Gradually, however, "going out lost some of its terrors." Eleanor began to develop a new circle of friends. "She wasn't a belle by any means," one of them recalled. "She was too tall for most of the young men. But she was an interesting talker. And she was always gracious and pleasant."

While people said that Eleanor was no beauty, her warm manner and lively mind quickly won admirers. Her eyes, said a friend, could melt anyone's heart, and her face, when animated, suddenly seemed lovely. Men and women alike found her sympathetic. At dinner parties, shrewd hostesses seated her next to older guests, because she could be counted on to make grown-up conversation.

A few months after Eleanor's debut, her grandmother decided to close her house in Manhattan and spend all her time in the country, where she could keep a close watch on Vallie. Eleanor went to live with a cousin, Susie Parish, and her family. By now, she had many friends in New York and had developed new interests. "I had grown up considerably during the past year," she wrote, "and had come to the conclusion that I would not spend another year just doing the social rounds."

As a debutante, Eleanor was automatically enrolled in the Junior

With her cousins Muriel Robbins (left) and Helen Roosevelt, June 1903.

League, an organization of wealthy young society women who "were anxious to do something helpful in the city in which we lived." One of the League's projects was to assist the settlement houses that offered classes and recreation in New York's teeming immigrant ghettos and slums. Junior League members gave fund-raising parties to help finance the settlement houses, but a few debutantes wanted to do more than simply raise money. They volunteered for active work in the slums. Eleanor decided to join this group.

With her friend Jean Reid, she taught classes at the Rivington Street Settlement House on Manhattan's Lower East Side. Jean played the piano, while Eleanor gave lessons in calisthenics and fancy dancing to the daughters of Jewish and Italian immigrants. Cousin Susie feared for Eleanor's safety on Rivington Street. And at first, "The dirty streets, crowded with foreign-looking people, filled me with terror," Eleanor admitted, ". . . but the children interested me enormously. I still remember the glow of pride that ran through me when one of the little girls said her father wanted me to come home with her, as he wanted to give me something because she enjoyed her classes so much."

Soon she enrolled in another reform group, the Consumers League, which was investigating working conditions among young female wage earners. The only working women Eleanor had ever met before were maids, cooks, and washerwomen at home and school. Now, accompanied by an experienced member of the League, she visited factories and department stores where young women worked twelve or fourteen hours a day, six days a week, for a weekly wage of six dollars.

When she was asked to visit some sweatshops where artificial flowers and feathers were made, "I was appalled. . . . I was frightened to death. But this is what had been required of me and I wanted to be useful. I entered my first sweatshop and walked up the steps of my first tenement. . . . I saw little children of four or five sitting at [work] tables until they dropped with fatigue."

At nineteen, Eleanor described herself as "a curious mixture of extreme innocence and unworldliness with a great deal of knowledge of some of the less agreeable sides of life." An enthusiastic volunteer, she became known as one of the outstanding members of the Junior League. But as she later acknowledged, "by spring I was ready to drop all this good work and go up to the country and spend the summer in idleness and recreation."

She had a special reason to look forward to summer that year. She had been seeing a particular young man, a handsome Harvard student who was even taller than she. He had asked for her hand, and she had accepted. They were secretly engaged.

Eleanor's engagement photo, 1904.

Franklin and Eleanor were secretly engaged when this photo was taken at Campobello Island in August 1904.

FOUR

Cousin Franklin

"I am so happy. Oh! so happy . . ."

One morning in the summer of 1902, Eleanor was riding the train to her grandmother's country house near Tivoli when she happened to meet her cousin Franklin Roosevelt. He spotted her as he was making his way down the aisle and stopped by her seat for a cheery hello.

Eleanor had just returned from school in England. Franklin was about to start his junior year at Harvard. They hadn't seen each other since Aunt Corinne's Christmas party three years earlier.

Franklin remembered Eleanor as a skinny girl in a hopeless party dress. Now she was wearing a stylish outfit from Paris. Tall but graceful, she had a glowing complexion, lustrous golden hair, and soft blue eyes that smiled up at him as he stood swaying above her in the aisle.

They were fifth cousins, once removed. Eleanor's father had been Franklin's godfather. And yet they scarcely knew each other. Growing up, they had met now and then at family gatherings.

Franklin and his mother, Sara, were on their way to their country estate at Hyde Park. He invited Eleanor to join them in the next car. Sara had lost her husband two years earlier and was still dressed entirely in black. Dark mourning veils hung from her hat to the floor. She greeted Eleanor cordially, and the three of them chatted until Franklin helped his mother off the train at the Hyde Park station.

That winter Eleanor made her debut. She began to run into Cousin
Franklin at debutante parties and dances. During the Christmas holidays,
he asked her to lunch in New York. On New Year's Day, 1903, they saw
each other again at the White House in Washington. While Eleanor was
away at school in England, her uncle Ted had been elected vice-president
of the United States on a ticket headed by William McKinley. A few
months later, McKinley was killed by an assassin's bullet and Theodore
Roosevelt became president.

As Roosevelt family members, Eleanor and Franklin both were invited
to the president's New Year's reception and dinner. A month later,
Eleanor helped celebrate Franklin's twenty-first birthday as one of the
guests at a festive dinner party in Hyde Park.

From then on, the shy, serious debutante and the jaunty, self-assured
Harvard man saw each other often. Franklin sought Eleanor's company.
He invited her to weekend house parties at Hyde Park, and to his mother's
summer cottage on Campobello Island off the coast of Maine. Eleanor
spent several days at Campobello with a group of other young people,
enjoying picnics, sailing expeditions, and walks along the cliffs overlooking the sea.

Of course, Eleanor and Franklin were never alone together. That would
have been highly improper in those formal Victorian days. When Eleanor
visited Hyde Park or Campobello, when she met Franklin in New York for
lunch or tea, even when they went riding in the Roosevelt carriage, a
third person was always present. If a relative wasn't available, Eleanor's
maid served as a chaperone.

Eleanor later described some of the strict rules that governed meetings
between single men and women in 1903: "It was understood that no girl
was interested in a man or showed any liking for him until he had made
all the advances. You knew a man very well before you wrote or received
a letter from him. . . . There were few men who would have dared to use
my first name, and to have signed oneself in any other way than 'very
sincerely yours' would have been not only a breach of good manners but
an admission of feeling which was entirely inadmissible.

"You never allowed a man to give you a present except flowers or candy

Wading at Campobello.

or possibly a book. To receive a piece of jewelry from a man to whom you were not engaged was a sign of being a fast woman, and the idea that you would permit any man to kiss you before you were engaged to him never even crossed my mind."

At first, Eleanor wondered if this princely young man-about-town, with his easy charm and exuberant high spirits, could seriously be interested in her. Franklin led a strenuous social life. He knew plenty of eligible young ladies. Eleanor feared that she might disappoint him, that she could not live up to his expectations. But Franklin did not lose interest, and as he persisted in his courtship, she opened her heart to him. He knew how to make her laugh. He was kind and attentive. He confided in her, asked her opinions and advice. When they were apart, she found that she missed him.

In November, Franklin invited Eleanor to attend the Harvard-Yale football game as his guest. She traveled to Boston on the train with an aunt and a cousin, who went along as chaperones. During the weekend, Eleanor and Franklin managed to slip away for a walk by themselves. By the time they returned, he had asked her to marry him and she had said yes.

Long afterward, Eleanor described that eventful walk to a close friend. Franklin had told her that "with your help" he was sure he would amount to something some day. And she had replied, "Why me? I am plain. I have little to bring you."

But Franklin, so earnest and handsome, persuaded Eleanor that he needed her. As his wife, she could stand beside him and help bring out all that was best in him. Her love and sense of purpose could help steady his own course in the years ahead.

Eleanor had dreamed of becoming a teacher like her beloved friend Marie Souvestre. And yet most people of that era believed that a woman's place was in the home. All of the young women Eleanor knew were already married or were planning to marry. As respectable society matrons, they would devote themselves to large households bustling with children and servants. "I felt the urge to be a part of the stream of life," Eleanor wrote, and when Franklin asked for her hand, "it seemed entirely natural and I never even thought that we were both young and inexperienced."

When Eleanor told her grandmother about Franklin's proposal, Mrs. Hall asked "if I was sure I was really in love. I solemnly answered 'yes,' and yet I know now it was years later before I understood what being in love or what loving really meant."

At the time, however, she had no doubts. "You are never out of my thoughts dear for one moment," she wrote to Franklin. "Everything is changed for me now. I am so happy. Oh! so happy & I love you *so* dearly."

Franklin shared the good news with his mother. "I am the happiest man just now in the world," he told her. "Likewise the luckiest."

Sara was stunned. She hadn't suspected that the courtship was serious.

Chatting with Franklin's mother. "I do hope she will learn to love me," said Eleanor.

Since her husband's death, she had devoted herself to Franklin. He was the center of her life, and she was not ready to give him up to marriage.

Sara did not object to Franklin's choice. Eleanor was a lovely girl *and* a Roosevelt—the niece of the president. But she was only nineteen. Franklin was twenty-one. Sara objected that they were too young to plunge into marriage. How could they be sure that they really cared enough? She asked them to keep their engagement secret for a year at least, to test their love and commitment. They agreed. "I realize more and more how hard it is for her," Eleanor told Franklin, "& we must both try always to make her happy & I do hope some day she will learn to love me."

As promised, they told no one for a full year while Franklin was

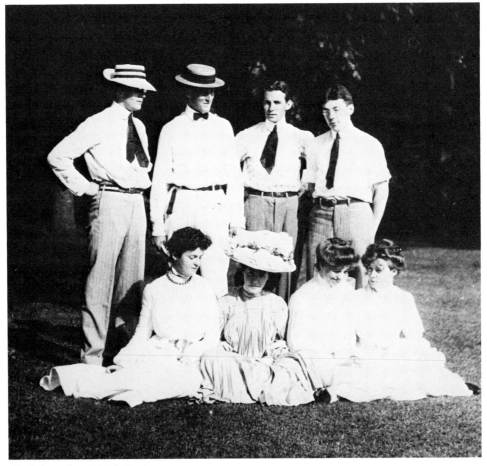

With friends at Hyde Park.

completing his final term at Harvard. They saw each other on weekends and holidays. Since they weren't officially engaged, a chaperone was still necessary whenever they were together.

They managed to keep their secret from friends and relatives who attended the same parties, dinners, and sporting events. But it seems that Eleanor was better at fooling people than Franklin. "I think he is very crazy about her, but she not about him," Cousin Corinne confided to her diary.

In public they had to be careful. But in their private letters they could express their feelings freely. "I am hungry for you every moment," Eleanor wrote, "you are never out of my thoughts, Dear."

And Franklin told his mother: "You can imagine how completely happy I am—it gives a stimulus to everything I do."

Eleanor, who had known so many fears of her own, understood Sara's fears of a lonely future. She did everything she could to reassure Sara, to win her love and acceptance. By the time the engagement was formally announced on December 1, 1904, the two women had become inseparable companions. Sara took "the dear child" shopping and lunching, to the theater and the opera, and for carriage rides through Central Park nearly every day.

Eleanor asked her uncle Ted—President Theodore Roosevelt—if he would stand in for her father at the wedding and give her away. The president replied that he would be *"dee-lighted!"* He often said that Eleanor was his "favorite niece." However, the wedding date would have to fit in with his presidential schedule. Finally it was decided that they would be married on March 17, 1905—St. Patrick's Day—since the president would be in New York to review the parade that day.

The ceremony took place in the candlelit drawing room of Cousin Susie's townhouse. Eleanor's satin wedding gown was covered with the same Brussels lace that both her mother and grandmother had worn at their own weddings. As the bride walked down the aisle—taller than the beaming president whose arm she held—guests who had known Anna Roosevelt turned to one another and murmured that, for once, Eleanor seemed to look like her beautiful mother.

Eleanor posed for her wedding portrait in a photographer's studio. No photographs were taken at the wedding ceremony.

The couple said their vows beneath a bower of palms and pink roses. Franklin lifted his bride's veil and kissed her. Then the president reached up to kiss his glowing niece. Turning to the groom he said, "Well, Franklin, there's nothing like keeping the name in the family."

Among the many messages of congratulation that day, a one-word cable arrived from England. It said *"Bonheur"* ("Happiness") and was signed "Souvestre."

The President Gives Away His Niece Eleanor in Marriage.

Mr. and Mrs. Roosevelt Attend the Wedding of His Late Brother's Daughter and Franklin Delano Roosevelt.

Cheers from East Seventy-sixth street at 3.30 o'clock sounded the approach of President Roosevelt, whose presence at the wedding of his niece, Miss Eleanor Roosevelt, and Franklin Delano Roosevelt, almost made the bride a secondary consideration. This wedding was celebrated in the twin homes of Mrs. Henry Parish, jr., and Mrs. E. Livingston Ludlow, Nos. 6 and 8 East Seventy-sixth street.

In the Name of the Father, and of the Son, and of the Holy Ghost, Amen.

Diocese of New York.

Church of the Incarnation,
New York City.

✝

This is to Certify

That *Franklin Delano Roosevelt*

and *Eleanor Roosevelt*

were united in

Holy Matrimony

according to the Rite of the Protestant Episcopal Church in the United States of America, and the Laws of the State of New York, on this *Seventeenth* day of *March* A.D. *1905*.

Rector.

Witnesses.

Theodore Roosevelt
Edith Kermit Roosevelt

What therefore God hath joined together let not man put asunder.—St. Mark x. 9.

The newlyweds spent a leisurely three-month honeymoon in Europe. They are seen here in Scotland, where they visited family friends.

Eleanor and Franklin with their first child, Anna. The dog, Duffy, was the first in a long line of Scotties in the Roosevelt family.

FIVE

A Conventional Society Matron

"As young women go, I suppose I was fitting pretty well into the pattern of a conventional, quiet young society matron."

After graduating from Harvard, Franklin enrolled in Columbia Law School in New York. He had to take his first year's exams before the newlyweds could leave for a belated three-month honeymoon in Europe.

They returned in September 1905—just in time for Franklin to resume his law studies. While they were away, his mother had rented a townhouse for them three blocks from her own. Sara furnished the house herself and staffed it with a cook, a butler, and a maid.

The following spring, Eleanor gave birth to their first child, a girl named Anna Eleanor after her mother and grandmother. Anna was the first of six babies that Eleanor would deliver. "For ten years," she wrote, "I was always just getting over having a baby or about to have one."

Franklin finished law school, passed his bar exams, and joined a Wall Street law firm. As was customary, he received no salary during his first year as an apprentice law clerk. Even so, his family did not lack for comforts. At a time when a working man earned about six hundred dollars a year, Franklin and Eleanor had a combined income of more than twelve thousand dollars from their inherited trust funds. And Sara was always ready to write a generous check on special occasions.

Eleanor slipped "with the greatest of ease" into the routine of a respectable society matron. Her mother-in-law came by every day in her carriage and the two ladies spent the afternoon together. Of course, Eleanor had never learned how to manage a household. Sara instructed her on every small domestic detail, from supervising the servants to planning formal dinners.

At Sara's insistence, Eleanor gave up her volunteer work. Her mother-in-law told her that "I had no right to go into the slums or into the hospitals, for fear of bringing diseases home to my children." Instead, she served on charitable boards and gave small sums to worthy causes.

Eleanor wanted to please Franklin's mother. She looked to Sara for advice and accepted her decisions on child care. Sara hired the nurses and nannies who changed the babies' diapers, fed them, and supervised them most of the day. "For years I was afraid of my nurses," Eleanor recalled, ". . . who ordered me around quite as much as they ordered the children."

After the birth of James, Eleanor's second baby, Sara decided to give the growing family a larger home. She bought a plot of land and hired an architect to build adjoining townhouses for herself and her "dear children." Sara and Franklin went over the plans together. "I left everything to my mother-in-law and my husband," Eleanor wrote. "I was growing dependent on my mother-in-law, requiring her help on almost every subject, and never thought of asking for anything that I thought would not meet with her approval."

When they moved, Eleanor felt disappointed and depressed. She hadn't wanted to live surrounded by servants, as the scale of the new house required. She never knew when Sara might suddenly appear, day or night, through the sliding doors that connected the drawing and dining rooms of the twin houses.

One evening Franklin came home to find his wife sitting at her dressing table and weeping: "When my bewildered young husband asked me what on earth was the matter with me, I said I did not like to live in a house which was not in any way mine, one that I had done nothing about and which did not represent the way I wanted to live."

Franklin asked why she hadn't spoken up before, when he had shown her the plans approved by him and his mother. He told her gently that she

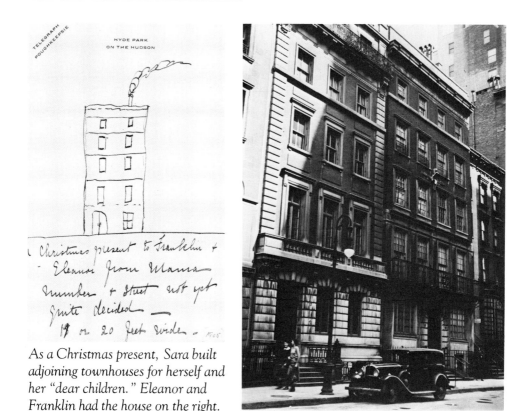

As a Christmas present, Sara built adjoining townhouses for herself and her "dear children." Eleanor and Franklin had the house on the right.

was "quite mad" and that she would feel better "in a little while." Then he quickly left the room.

"I pulled myself together and realized I was acting like a little fool," Eleanor wrote, "but there was a good deal of truth in what I had said, for I was not developing any individual taste or initiative. I was simply absorbing the personalities of those about me and letting their tastes and interests dominate me."

The couple's third child, Franklin, Jr., was the "biggest and most beautiful of all the babies." He seemed to be thriving, but in the fall of 1909, when he was seven months old, he came down with the flu. His parents and the doctors watched helplessly as the infant failed and died. "Poor E.'s mother heart is well nigh broken," Sara wrote in her journal. "She so hoped and cannot believe her baby is gone from her . . . my heart aches for Eleanor."

Eleanor could not accept the baby's loss, and in her grief she blamed herself: "I felt he had been left too much to the nurse, and I knew too little about him, and that in some way I must be to blame. I even felt that I had not cared enough about him, and I made myself and all those around me most unhappy during that winter. I was even a little bitter against my poor young husband who occasionally tried to make me see how idiotically I was behaving."

Franklin grieved for the baby, too. Ten months after the infant's death, another son, Elliott, was born.

During these early years of their marriage, Eleanor and Franklin discovered that they were very different in ways that mattered to them both. Eleanor could never be as lighthearted as her fun-loving husband may have wished. "Duty," she wrote, "was perhaps the motivating force of my life, often excluding what might have been joy or pleasure. I looked at

Sara pours tea aboard the family yacht Half Moon. *With her are three-year-old Anna and Eleanor.*

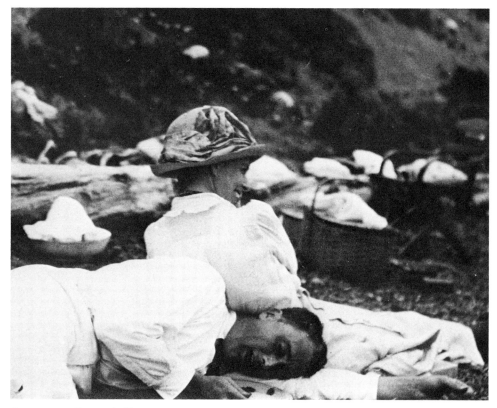

A picnic at Campobello.

everything from the point of view of what I ought to do, rarely from the standpoint of what I wanted to do. . . . I was never carefree. . . ."

As a girl, Eleanor had learned to keep her resentments and disappointments to herself. When she was angry or hurt, she retreated into silence, "shutting up like a clam, not telling anyone what is the matter . . . feeling like a martyr and acting like one." Franklin was often puzzled by her moods. His way of dealing with unpleasant problems was to laugh them off, to pretend they didn't exist. He hated to see his wife withdrawn and depressed, but when she was, he would simply leave her alone until it blew over.

For all their differences, Eleanor concentrated on making their marriage a success. Her family provided a comforting sense of security that she had not known when she was growing up. Some of their friends worried that she gave in too easily to her mother-in-law—she was always saying, "Yes, Mama," or "No, Mama" (with the accent on the last syllable). It was a price Eleanor was willing to pay. She had Franklin's love and her home, and that was what counted.

"Dearest Honey," she wrote once when Franklin was away, "I miss you dreadfully and feel very lonely, but please don't think it is because I am alone, having other people wouldn't do any good for I just want you!"

Bored with his Wall Street law firm, Franklin wanted to enter politics. He dreamed of following in the footsteps of his cousin Theodore, who had served as a state legislator, assistant secretary of the navy, governor of New York, and finally, as the nation's president.

His chance came in 1910, when Democratic Party leaders in Dutchess County, where Hyde Park was located, invited him to run for the New York State Senate. Franklin was a personable young man from a prominent local family. He had enough money to finance his own campaign in a solidly Republican district. No one believed that he had a chance to win, but he was eager to test himself.

Eleanor—now twenty-six and the mother of three—supported her husband's ambitions. "I listened to all his plans with a great deal of interest," she wrote. "It never occurred to me that I had any part to play. I felt that I must acquiesce in whatever he might decide and be willing to go to Albany."

To everyone's surprise, Franklin won the election. Eleanor looked forward to living in Albany, the state capital, where she would get away from her mother-in-law for a change. While her husband served his first term as a state senator, she did her best to be a model politician's wife. She wrote that she took an interest in politics because "It was a wife's duty to be interested in whatever interested her husband, whether it was politics, books, or a particular dish for dinner."

Their rented house in Albany became a popular meeting place for Franklin's fellow politicians. Eleanor was the gracious hostess who served snacks and refreshments night after night. During the day she called on the wives of other freshman legislators and the wives of local newspaper-

*Eleanor accompanies
her husband as he
campaigns for the
New York State
Senate in 1910.*

men, making friends for Franklin all over town. In New York, the
Roosevelts' social life had been restricted to a narrow circle of wealthy
families. In the state capital, Eleanor met men and women from a wide
range of backgrounds. "I was beginning to get interested in human
beings," she wrote, "and I found that almost everyone had something
interesting to contribute to my education."

Of course, everyone in Albany talked endlessly about politics. Eleanor
listened to countless political discussions in her own home. She sat in the
visitors' gallery of the state senate and followed the debates. She discussed

A growing family. Eleanor with James, Elliott, and Anna, June 1911.

issues with Franklin. And yet in her mind, politics was a man's business. When Franklin came out in favor of women's suffrage—granting American women the right to vote—Eleanor was "shocked." "I had never given the matter serious thought," she admitted, "for I took it for granted that men were superior creatures and knew more about politics than women did." She decided "that if my husband was a suffragist I probably must be, too."

Eleanor wanted to support Franklin's political career and share his interests, but her own life centered on her family. By now she had become the accomplished manager of a large household, proud of the many tasks she crowded into her daily schedule as a mother, a society matron, and a political wife. With a minimum of fuss, she supervised the family's frequent moves between Albany, Hyde Park, New York City, and Campobello—the children, their nurses, four or five other servants, a mountain of trunks, valises, and hatboxes, and an assortment of pets. A friend called the procession "an army on the move."

In 1912, Franklin won a second term in the state senate. He also had his first taste of national politics that year, supporting Woodrow Wilson, a progressive Democrat, as the party's candidate for president. Wilson was elected. Soon afterward, State Senator Roosevelt, barely thirty-one years old, was invited to Washington, D.C., and appointed assistant secretary of the navy. Once again the family moved, this time to a rented house in the nation's capital.

Eleanor took on a new set of duties. Wearing white gloves and a fashionable hat, she spent her weekday afternoons making formal calls on the wives of congressmen, cabinet members, and diplomats. After each day's round of calls, prominent women would tell their husbands that Mrs. Franklin D. Roosevelt, wife of the assistant secretary of the navy, had paid her respects. "My shyness was wearing off rapidly," wrote Eleanor.

The Roosevelts became a popular twosome—"the most attractive and nicest young couple I know," said a Washington hostess. Franklin was regarded as one of the handsomest men in town. Eleanor was "far less striking" but was "cordial and charming." "We lived a kind of social life I had never known before," she wrote, "dining out night after night and having people dine with us about once a week."

Their social schedule was too much for Eleanor to handle alone. She spent so much time arranging her calling list, answering and sending invitations, that she finally hired a social secretary, a vivacious young woman named Lucy Mercer. Lucy became a friend of the family. She often ate with the Roosevelts, and when Eleanor needed an extra woman for a formal dinner party, she invited Lucy.

Informally, Eleanor and Franklin met for Sunday supper every two weeks with a small group of friends. One of them, William Phillips, an assistant secretary of state, recalled Franklin as "a brilliant, lovable, and somewhat happy-go-lucky friend. . . . His wife, Eleanor, whom we all admired, was a quiet member of our little group. She seemed to be a little

Lucy Mercer.

remote, or it may have been that Franklin claimed the attention, leaving her somewhat in the background."

During those years in Washington, Eleanor gave birth to two more children—the second Franklin, Jr., in 1914, and John, the baby of the family, in 1916. Anna, James, and Elliott were in school now. Early in her marriage, Eleanor had allowed the children's nurses and governesses a free hand. But with five growing youngsters in the house, she was no longer a timid, inexperienced mother, and she took a direct hand in the children's upbringing.

Franklin loved to romp with his "chicks." He took them on outings and indulged them, but he shrank from disciplining them. Their grandmother spoiled them at every opportunity. It was left to Eleanor to lecture the children when they failed to study, or to scold or punish them when they misbehaved. Years later, she felt that she had been too strict, and she regretted it. "I was certainly not an ideal mother," she wrote. "Playing with children was difficult for me because play had not been an important part of my own childhood."

Her son James agreed. "I don't think Mother shared in the day-to-day fun in life at all in things like skating, sledding, etc.," he reminisced. "She was very good about making arrangements, but she did not participate. We had more real fun with Mother when we were all much older. . . ."

During these years, war had broken out in Europe between the Allies, a group of countries led by Britain and France, and the Central Powers, dominated by Imperial Germany. At first the United States remained neutral, but President Wilson, along with many other Americans, sympathized with the Allies. When German submarines began to attack Allied and neutral shipping in the Atlantic, sinking three American ships, it became apparent that the United States would be drawn into the conflict.

"There was a sense of impending disaster hanging over all of us," Eleanor recalled. "The various attacks on our shipping were straining our relations with Germany and more and more the temper of the country was turning against the Germans. . . . After weeks of tension, I heard that the President was going to address Congress as a preliminary to a declaration of war. Everyone wanted to hear this historic address and it was with the greatest difficulty that Franklin got me a seat. I listened breathlessly and returned home half dazed by the sense of impending change."

On April 6, 1917, the United States entered World War I as an ally of Britain and France. For the first time in history, American combat troops would be shipped overseas to fight in Europe.

"From then on," Eleanor wrote, "the men in the government worked from morning until late into the night. The women in Washington paid no more calls. They began to organize at once to meet the unusual demands of wartime." At the Navy Department, assistant secretary Franklin Roosevelt directed the mobilization of America's naval bases and warships. Eleanor wanted to do her part, and she plunged into voluntary war work: "Instead of making calls, I found myself spending three days a week in a canteen down at the railroad yards, one afternoon a week distributing [yarn] for the Navy League, two days a week visiting the naval hospital, and contributing whatever time I had left to the Navy Red Cross and the Navy Relief Society."

Millions of American women rallied to the war effort. Many women took over jobs usually held by men, working as mechanics, telegraph operators, and mail carriers. Eleanor became one of seventy thousand women who volunteered to work at Red Cross canteens in the nation's railroad stations, where servicemen on the move could line up for soup, sandwiches, coffee, postcards, and a friendly smile.

She was assigned to the canteen in Washington's Union Station. During the hot and steamy summer of 1918, when many volunteers were away on vacation, she often rose at five A.M. to go to the canteen—"do not you think that mother should not go so early?" James complained in a note to his grandmother. One busy morning she cut her finger to the bone while using the bread-slicing machine. "There was no time to stop," she recalled, "so I wrapped something tightly around it and proceeded during the day to wrap more and more handkerchiefs around it, until it finally stopped bleeding." She didn't see a doctor until that evening, and she carried the scar for the rest of her life.

Eleanor had volunteered out of a sense of duty, and yet her war work

Eleanor accompanies her husband as he inspects the New York navy yards, April 1913.

By 1916, when John was born, the family was complete. Shown with their parents are Elliott (born in 1910), Franklin, Jr. (1914), James (1907), John, and Anna (1906).

brought unexpected satisfactions. It was the first time since her marriage that she had ventured outside the family circle. She found that she enjoyed taking on new tasks and meeting new people. "I loved it," she said later. "I simply ate it up."

No job was too troublesome or distasteful for her. She was as willing to scrub the canteen floor as she was to organize committees and supervise other volunteers. Her fellow workers called her a "dynamo." "I was learning to have a certain confidence in myself and in my ability to meet emergencies and deal with them," she wrote.

The Red Cross wanted to send her to England, where she would set up canteens for American servicemen. It was quite a temptation, but she wasn't willing to leave her family and travel abroad by herself.

Franklin did go overseas that summer on an official mission to inspect American naval bases in Europe and tour the fighting fronts. He returned to New York two months later suffering from double pneumonia. He was so weak that he had to be carried off the ship on a stretcher and taken home in an ambulance. Eleanor hurried to New York to look after her ailing husband.

One afternoon as Franklin slept, she was putting away some of his things when she found a bundle of letters addressed to her husband. She recognized the handwriting instantly. They were from Lucy Mercer, Eleanor's social secretary and family friend. She could see at a glance that they were love letters.

Eleanor with John and Franklin, Jr., 1919.

SIX

The Education of Eleanor Roosevelt

"The bottom dropped out of my own particular world and I faced myself, my surroundings, my world, honestly for the first time. I really grew up that year."

When Eleanor found Lucy Mercer's love letters, she knew with a sinking heart that life would never be the same again. After thirteen years of marriage and six children, she felt that Franklin had discarded her for a younger, more attractive woman.

She confronted her feverish, bedridden husband and offered him his "freedom." She was not willing to endure a marriage in which she felt merely tolerated. She would step aside. Franklin could have a divorce, if that was what he wanted.

Franklin's mother was horrified! In those days, even the *idea* of divorce was scandalous. Sara Roosevelt told her son that if he really wished to abandon his wife and *her* grandchildren for that woman, she could not stop him. But she made it perfectly clear that she would cut him off without a penny of his inheritance.

Franklin's close friend and adviser, Louis Howe, went back and forth trying to patch things up. He warned Franklin that the disgrace of a divorce would put an end to his political career. He pleaded with Eleanor to think of the children's welfare and her own future, and to forgive her husband.

In the end, Eleanor and Franklin agreed to hold their marriage together.

They remained a family. According to their daughter, Anna, Franklin "voluntarily promised to end any 'romantic relationship' with Lucy and seemed to realize how much pain he had given [Eleanor]."

Franklin had wavered. Now he wanted to make amends. He cared about his wife. He was sorry he had hurt her. Eleanor did her best to respond, but she could not shake off her feelings of humiliation and betrayal. Never again would she allow herself to be taken for granted.

Though she and Franklin reconciled, their relationship had changed forever. It became more a partnership than a marriage—a very close and affectionate partnership based on mutual interests and a shared past, but without the intimacy of marriage. Years later Eleanor told friends, "I have the memory of an elephant. I can forgive but I can never forget."

World War I—"the war to end all wars"—ended with the signing of the Armistice on November 11, 1918. "The city of Washington, like every other city in the United States, went completely mad," Eleanor recalled. "The feeling of relief and thankfulness was beyond description." It had been the bloodiest and most destructive war ever fought. Some ten million soldiers from many countries had lost their lives. More than twenty million had been wounded.

As assistant navy secretary, Franklin was responsible for closing down American naval bases overseas. He asked Eleanor to return to Europe with him—their first ocean voyage since their honeymoon. Wherever they traveled on the Continent that winter, they saw the grim effects of total warfare. In Paris, it seemed to Eleanor that "practically every French woman was dressed in black." Out in the countryside, they visited scarred and silent battlefields where, months before, thousands of young men had been shelled, shot, gassed, and bayoneted to death. "We drove along the straight military roads with churned mud on either side of us, and deep shell holes here and there," wrote Eleanor. "Along the road there were occasional piles of stones with a stick stuck into them bearing the name of a vanished village. On the hillsides stumps showed that once there had been a forest."

In February 1919, the Roosevelts sailed back to America aboard the

Returning from Europe aboard the U.S.S. George Washington, *February 1919. Much remained unspoken.*

same ship as President and Mrs. Wilson, who were returning from a triumphant tour of France. At the Paris Peace Conference, Wilson had persuaded Allied leaders to accept his plan for a League of Nations, an international organization that would help maintain a lasting peace. "What hopes we had that this League would really prove the instrument for the prevention of future wars," Eleanor wrote.

Back home in Washington, Eleanor managed her household, supervised her children's schooling, and met her social obligations. And she continued to find satisfaction in her volunteer work. During the war she had handed out sandwiches and a smile to soldiers heading for the front. Now she spent several days a week visiting wounded and shell-shocked veterans at St. Elizabeth's Hospital.

She kept busy, and yet the spring and summer of 1919 were a trying period for her. Her faith in herself had been shaken by the Lucy Mercer affair, and at times she was overcome by dark moods of depression and despair. "I do not think I have ever felt so strangely as in the past year," she confided in her diary, ". . . all my self-confidence is gone and I am on edge though I never was better physically I feel sure."

For the first time, she began to stand up to her mother-in-law. More than once, harsh words passed between the two women. "Mama and I have had a bad time," Eleanor noted in her diary. "I should be ashamed of myself and I'm not."

With Franklin, there were strained silences and angry flare-ups. Much remained unspoken. And yet mutual pain seemed to strengthen the bond between them. Franklin did everything he could think of to please Eleanor. She made an effort to be a more relaxed and carefree companion. "Last night's party was really wonderful and I enjoyed it," she told Sara. ". . . I actually danced once." Not since the early days of their marriage had they spent so much time together. When Franklin was away, she missed him. When they were together, she was easily upset.

"I wish we did not lead such a hectic life," she wrote to him in the autumn of 1919, "a little prolonged quiet might bring us together & yet it might do just the opposite! I really don't know what I want or think about anything anymore!"

In 1920, Franklin resigned from the Navy Department so he could enter national politics. The Democrats had nominated Ohio Governor James M. Cox as their presidential candidate to succeed Woodrow Wilson. Cox picked thirty-eight-year-old Franklin Roosevelt as his running mate. While the Democrats were given little chance of winning that year, Franklin jumped at the chance to gain political experience and become widely known.

The big issue was whether or not the United States should join the newly created League of Nations. Cox and Roosevelt spoke out strongly in favor of the League. The Republican candidates, Warren G. Harding and Calvin Coolidge, refused to support American membership. After a costly war overseas, they called for "a return to normalcy" at home.

The Education of Eleanor Roosevelt

Mrs. James Cox and Eleanor Roosevelt watch their candidate husbands from a reviewing stand during the presidential campaign of 1920.

The 1920 election would be the first national election in which women could vote. A candidate's wife was suddenly important, and Franklin wanted Eleanor at his side. He asked her to join him aboard his campaign train. Dutifully, she became the only woman among the aides and newspapermen who accompanied the candidate on a four-week swing across the country.

At every whistle-stop along the way, Franklin enthusiastically greeted the crowds from the rear platform of the train. Eleanor found herself listening to the same speech over and over again. "It is becoming almost impossible to stop F. now when he begins to speak," she wrote to Sara. If Franklin went on too long, his aides would wave at him from the rear of the crowd. "When nothing else succeeds I yank his coattails!" Eleanor reported.

During the trip, Eleanor found an ally in Franklin's friend and adviser Louis Howe. A former newspaper reporter and a shrewd political observer, Louis had met Franklin in Albany and followed him to Washington to serve as his assistant at the Navy Department. He was convinced that Franklin could become president someday.

Eleanor had never liked Howe—a rumpled, gnomelike, chain-smoking little man who slouched beside her husband like his political shadow and claimed to possess one of the four ugliest faces in New York. On the campaign train, she discovered that Howe's looks were deceiving. Beneath the surface, he was a sensitive and perceptive man.

Louis Howe, Franklin's friend and political adviser. Eleanor's opinion of Howe changed during the 1920 campaign.

The campaign schedule was grueling. At the end of each strenuous day, Franklin and his aides would gather in the back of a pullman car and relax—playing poker, telling jokes, plotting the next day's strategy. Howe saw that Eleanor felt like an outsider. He sensed her unhappiness, her uncertainty about her role as a candidate's wife. One evening he went to Eleanor and told her that she could make a real contribution to Franklin's campaign. He began to discuss Franklin's speeches with her, and he asked for her ideas and opinions on a wide range of campaign issues. Eleanor was grateful to him. By the end of the trip, they had become fast friends.

As expected, the Democrats lost that year. Republican Warren Harding was elected president, and American membership in the League of Nations became a dead issue.

For the first time in a decade, Franklin Roosevelt was out of public life. He and Eleanor moved back to New York, where Franklin joined a law firm and began to plan his next political move.

By now, Eleanor had made up her mind that she was going to be more independent. She was no longer willing to stay quietly in the background while her husband had all the fun. "I did not look forward to a winter . . . in New York with nothing but teas and luncheons and dinners to take up my time," she wrote. She enrolled in a business school and took courses in shorthand and typing. And she joined a new organization, the League of Women Voters, founded in 1920 by veterans of the long battle for women's suffrage.

When Eleanor volunteered to work for the League, she was asked to serve on the legislative committee, which reported to the membership on proposed new laws. At first she was reluctant. She felt she knew little about the mysteries of legislation. Promised the assistance of an attorney named Elizabeth Read, she agreed to take on the job. "I felt humble and inadequate when I first presented myself to Elizabeth Read," she recalled, "but I liked her at once and she gave me a sense of confidence."

Eleanor soon met Esther Lape, a college professor and writer who also worked for the League and who shared a house in Greenwich Village with Elizabeth Read. "Esther had a brilliant mind and driving force, a kind of nervous power," Eleanor wrote. "Elizabeth seemed calmer, more practical and domestic, but I came to see that hers was a keen and analytical mind and in its way as brilliant as Esther's. . . . Their standards of work and their interests played a great part in what might be called the 'intensive education of Eleanor Roosevelt' during the next few years."

Eleanor admired these two gifted women who were so different from the conventional society matrons she had always known. She began to spend stimulating evenings at their home, meeting interesting new people, discussing art, poetry, politics, and the future of America. Meanwhile, her willingness to work and her good sense impressed her fellow volunteers at the League of Women Voters. Before long, Eleanor was playing an important role in the organization, drafting bills and making policy.

"My mother-in-law was distressed because I was not always available, as I had been when I lived in New York before," she wrote. "I had long ceased to be dependent on my mother-in-law. . . . I was thinking things out for myself and becoming an individual."

Esther Lape and Elizabeth Read played a major role in Eleanor's political awakening.

On the beach at Campobello before Franklin's illness.

The summer of 1921 found the Roosevelts and their guests enjoying the breezy pleasures of Campobello Island. One afternoon in August, after an outing and a swim, Franklin complained of a chill and went to bed early. He awoke the next morning with a high fever, stabbing pains in his back and legs, and a creeping paralysis.

Soon he could not stand up or move his legs. Puzzled, the local doctor called in a colleague from Bar Harbor, Maine. Finally a specialist came up from Newport, Rhode Island. The diagnosis was alarming. Franklin had been stricken with polio—infantile paralysis. He was paralyzed from the waist down.

At the time, there was no vaccine for polio and no effective cure. Franklin lay in his sickroom with the shades drawn, uncertain whether he would ever walk again. For nearly three weeks, until a trained nurse could be brought up from New York, Eleanor slept on a couch in his room, nursing him and comforting him day and night, spelled only by Louis Howe. Together they bathed Franklin, massaged his back and legs, and attended to his every need.

Despite his agony and fears, Franklin managed to put up a cheerful front. When the frightened children peered into the darkened room, he would wave at them and smile and say something to make them laugh. As Eleanor cared for him, lying there so helplessly, the hurt and resentment that had colored her feelings gave way to tenderness and compassion for her suffering husband.

Franklin was finally moved to a hospital in New York, a painful and difficult journey from Campobello by boat, train, and ambulance. After weeks of therapy, he was allowed to go home. But his legs were still paralyzed. The vigorous young attorney who had raced his children to the beach and bounded up the steps of his office three at a time could not walk a single step.

He concentrated on the exercises that he hoped would overcome his paralysis. Louis Howe moved into the Roosevelts' Manhattan townhouse to keep Franklin company and help handle his business affairs. With five children, the servants, and a full-time nurse for Franklin, the house was full, leaving Eleanor without a room of her own. "I slept on a bed in one of the little boys' rooms," she wrote, "I dressed in my husband's bathroom. In the daytime I was too busy to need a room."

Franklin's mother had made up her mind that her son would be handicapped for the rest of his life. She wanted him to retire to Hyde Park, where he could lead a sheltered life of leisure under his mother's watchful eyes. "Her anxiety over his general health was so great that she dreaded his making any effort whatsoever," Eleanor wrote. "She always thought that she understood what was best, particularly where her child was concerned, regardless of what any doctor might say."

But Eleanor and Louis were determined that Franklin should not be defeated by his illness. They wanted him to take an active part in life again, to go back to work as soon as he was able. While Franklin struggled to regain the use of his legs, they would join forces to keep his political and business contacts alive.

Eleanor refused to treat Franklin as an invalid, and she would not allow others to do so. She argued bitterly with her mother-in-law over Franklin's future. Sara was furious. She dismissed Louis as "that ugly, dirty little

Supporting himself on crutches, Franklin greets Democratic presidential candidate John W. Davis, August 1924.

man" and tried to enlist the children to side with her. Once, Eleanor became so angry that she blocked the sliding doors connecting their twin townhouses by pushing a heavy breakfront against the doorway. "In many ways this was the most trying winter of my entire life," she wrote.

One afternoon she was reading to Franklin, Jr., and John, the two youngest boys, when she broke into sobs. She could not go on with the story: "I could not think why I was sobbing, nor could I stop. Elliott came in from school, dashed in to look at me and fled. Mr. Howe came in and tried to find out what the matter was, but he gave it up as a bad job. The two little boys went off to bed and I sat on the sofa in the sitting room and sobbed and sobbed. . . . Finally I found an empty room in my mother-in-law's house, as she had moved to the country. I locked the door and poured cold water on a towel and mopped my face. Eventually I pulled myself together. . . .

"This is the one and only time I remember in my entire life having gone to pieces in this particular manner. From that time on I seemed to have got rid of nerves and uncontrollable tears. . . ."

That winter, with Louis close at hand to bolster her resolve, Eleanor freed herself once and for all from her mother-in-law's domination. Franklin's illness, she said, "made me stand on my own two feet in regard to my husband's life, my own life, and my children's training." If she had given in to Sara, she believed, she would have become "a completely colorless echo of my husband and mother-in-law and torn between them. I might have stayed a weak character forever if I had not found that out."

Franklin's encounter with polio changed him. For the first time in his life, he had suffered the agonies of pain and terror in a way that he had never imagined possible. He had discovered what it was like to be weak and helpless, to be totally dependent on others. "Franklin's illness proved a blessing in disguise," wrote Eleanor, "for it gave him strength and courage he had not had before. He had to think out the fundamentals of living and learn the greatest of all lessons—infinite patience and never-ending persistence."

His illness had changed Eleanor, too. Like Franklin, she emerged from the ordeal tested and toughened.

On the porch at Hyde Park, six years after Franklin was paralyzed by polio.

*Esther Lape and Eleanor Roosevelt on their way to
a congressional hearing in Washington.*

❧ SEVEN ❧

Friendship and Politics

"If anyone were to ask me what I want out of life I would say—the opportunity for doing something useful, for in no other way, I am convinced, can true happiness be attained."

For years after he was stricken, Franklin believed that he would walk again. He focused his energies on the exercises and therapy that he hoped would restore the use of his legs.

Louis Howe urged Eleanor to act as her husband's stand-in. While Franklin concentrated on his recovery, she could help keep the Roosevelt name in the public eye. Eleanor had already shown a knack for politics at the League of Women Voters. She welcomed this new chance to involve herself in public life. "I'm only being *active* until you can be again," she assured Franklin.

She joined the newly organized women's division of the New York State Democratic Party and moved swiftly into positions of leadership. With Louis's encouragement and advice, she took on a job as editor and advertising manager of a monthly publication, the *Women's Democratic News,* writing editorials and many articles herself. And she traveled all over the state, helping to set up local Democratic clubs for women. A coworker, Molly Dewson, praised Eleanor's "human warmth, sincerity, and genuine interest in other persons."

Eleanor enjoyed meeting people, but she was terrified of speaking in public. In conversation, her voice was warm and relaxed. Before an audience, she trembled. She was so self-conscious that her voice wavered and rose several octaves, while her speech was punctuated by nervous giggles.

Louis offered to coach her. When she spoke, he sat at the back of the hall and studied her manner and delivery. He didn't hesitate to criticize Eleanor, or to tell her how "inane" her giggle sounded. His advice was: "Have something to say, say it, and then sit down."

Her speaking style improved. Word spread that she was a woman with interesting views and the ability to present them effectively. Democratic leaders invited her to present the party's viewpoint in debates, on the lecture circuit, and over the radio—a new and powerful force in American life. As Eleanor's reputation grew, newspapers called her for statements. Magazines asked her to write articles.

She took pride and pleasure in the work she was doing, but she learned that politics was still very much a man's game. In New York, women were

At the Democratic National Convention in 1924, Mrs. Roosevelt addresses the party's newly formed women's division.

welcome to form their own division of the Democratic Party. They were encouraged to work for political candidates. But when it came to selecting nominees and setting policy, the men who ran the party were clearly in charge.

At the Democratic National Convention in 1924, Eleanor Roosevelt was asked to chair a women's subcommittee that conducted hearings and suggested planks to the official resolutions committee. And yet the men who ran the resolutions committee had no real interest in hearing from these "lady politicians." During meetings of the men's committee, Eleanor and her colleagues had to stand outside the closed doors of the committee room and wait for hours before anyone would even accept their proposals. Afterward, she never knew if their proposals had actually been discussed.

"I [saw] for the first time where women stood when it came to a national convention," she wrote later. "They stood outside the door of all important meetings and waited."

As Eleanor worked with women's groups around the state, she made many new friends. She became part of a growing circle of reform-minded, politically savvy women—teachers, lawyers, union organizers, and social activists who had strong convictions and progressive goals. They were fighting to win a forty-eight-hour work week for women, a fair minimum wage, the end of child labor, and the right of women to organize into trade unions. In political affairs, they wanted women to have an equal voice with men. Suddenly, they were the most interesting people whom Eleanor knew.

She drew especially close to Marion Dickerman and Nancy Cook, two of her associates from the women's division of the Democratic Party. Marion and Nan had lived and worked together for many years. During World War I they had gone overseas as nursing orderlies and served in a London hospital. After the war, Marion had run for the New York State Assembly—the first woman in the state to seek a legislative office. Nan was her campaign manager. Although Marion lost, the two friends remained active in Democratic politics. Eleanor relied on their guidance when she joined the party's women's division.

Nancy Cook (second from left) and Marion Dickerman (right) became Eleanor's closest friends. They are shown with Marion's sister Peggy Levenson in front of Eleanor's seven-passenger touring car, July 1926.

Marion and Nan became Eleanor's constant companions. Franklin liked both of them. He enjoyed their company and listened seriously to their ideas. They were the sort of people a politician should know.

One weekend in 1924, Franklin, Eleanor, Marion, and Nan spread a picnic on the grassy bank of Val-Kill Creek, about two miles east of the Roosevelt mansion at Hyde Park. They had picked a beautiful spot on a glorious autumn day. Eleanor reminded everyone that it would be their last picnic of the year, since Franklin's mother soon would be closing the Hyde Park house for the winter.

Although Sara owned the estate at Hyde Park, Franklin had purchased some land around Val-Kill Creek for himself. He suggested that Eleanor, Marion, and Nan build a cottage for themselves on that very spot. Marion and Nan could live there year-round if they liked, and Eleanor could join them whenever she wished.

Franklin sympathized with Eleanor's wish to be independent of his mother. The big house at Hyde Park was Sara's domain. Eleanor had never felt truly at home there. She needed a place of her own where she could relax with her friends without having to negotiate with her mother-in-law.

"My Missus and some of her female political friends want to build a shack on a stream in the backwoods," Franklin told a friend. He hired an architect and personally supervised the construction of a handsome fieldstone cottage, modeled after old Dutch houses. The creek was dammed to form a pond, and its water diverted for a swimming pool where Franklin could exercise his paralyzed legs in private. On New Year's Day of 1926, Val-Kill Cottage was inaugurated with a festive dinner party attended by the entire Roosevelt family. Everyone sat on kegs of nails, including Sara.

Eleanor loved the place. "The peace of it is divine," she told Franklin.

Nancy Cook, a skilled cabinetmaker, designed and built much of the furniture for the new house. It turned out so well that the three friends decided to start a small furniture factory in a building near their cottage, supervised by Nancy. Until it finally closed during the Great Depression, the factory hired local people to craft handmade reproductions of early American pieces.

Marion Dickerman was a teacher and vice-principal at the Todhunter School in Manhattan, a private school for girls. At her invitation, Eleanor began to teach classes in literature, drama, and American history. When Marion was offered a chance to purchase the school, Eleanor suggested that they buy it together. "Teaching gave her some of the happiest moments of her life," said Marion. "She loved it. The girls worshipped her."

Along with teaching and politics, Eleanor found time to be both mother and father to her children. Franklin was constantly away, seeking a cure for his paralysis. In 1926, he bought a rundown resort at Warm Springs, Georgia, where the soothing mineral waters seemed to help his wasted leg muscles. Eventually, he turned the resort into a rehabilitation center for polio victims. Warm Springs became his second home.

Eleanor was the parent who took the boys to boarding school each fall, met with their teachers and counselors, and attended functions for parents. She wanted Franklin, Jr., and John to have the same experiences they would have enjoyed with their father, if he were not paralyzed. "I had two young boys who had to learn to do the things that boys must do—swim, ride, and camp," she wrote. "It began to dawn on me that if these two youngest boys were going to have a normal existence without a father to do these things with them, I would have to become a good deal more companionable and more of an all-round person than I had ever been before."

Franklin would have taught the boys to swim. As a girl, Eleanor had been afraid of the water. She had never learned to swim properly. Now, a woman of forty, she took swimming lessons at the YWCA pool in New York one winter so she could in turn teach her young sons.

Wrestling with daughter Anna at Val-Kill.

On the dock at Campobello with Franklin, Jr., and John.

She also took lessons to improve her driving, so she could take the boys on motor tours and camping trips. One summer Eleanor, Nan, Marion, Franklin, Jr., Johnny, and two other youngsters all set out in Eleanor's seven-passenger Buick on a camping trip to Canada, carrying two tents, cooking gear, and a Red Cross first aid kit. Where there were no public camping sites, they set up their tents in farmers' fields each evening as they traveled north along the St. Lawrence River toward Quebec. On the way home they camped in New Hampshire, where they all climbed the White Mountains on burros.

In 1928, Democratic Party leaders persuaded Franklin Roosevelt to end his exile and return to politics as a candidate for governor of New York. Roosevelt's legs were still paralyzed and would remain so for the rest of his life. He had to wear steel and leather leg braces that locked at the knees. Even then, he could not stand or walk without crutches or the help of a cane and someone's arm. Except for that, he was a vigorous, healthy man. He campaigned throughout New York State, traveling by automobile and train and making several speeches a day.

Although the Republicans swept the national elections that year, Roosevelt won a narrow victory in New York. Once again, Franklin and Eleanor moved to the state capital at Albany. This time, they set up housekeeping in the governor's mansion.

Eleanor had mixed feelings about her new role as First Lady of New York State. By now she was a political power in her own right. While Franklin ran for governor, she served as codirector of the Democratic Party's National Women's Committee—making her one of the best-known and highest-ranking Democrats in the country. She was happy that her husband could return to public life. As the governor's wife, however, she would be expected to stay in the background.

"I know if I take any part in politics everyone will attribute anything I say or do to Franklin and that wouldn't be fair to him," she said. Regretfully, she resigned from her official party posts. But she found ways to stay active and influential behind the scenes.

Meanwhile, she managed to combine teaching with her obligations in

Inauguration Day, January 1, 1929. The new governor poses for a formal portrait with his wife and mother.

the governor's mansion. She commuted to Manhattan by train on Sunday evening, met her classes at Todhunter School the first three days of the week, and returned to Albany late Wednesday afternoon. During the train ride, she read students' papers and worked on lesson plans. "I teach because I love it," she said. "I cannot give it up."

Every week she could be seen clutching a bulging briefcase and running through the station at the last minute. She was always surprised when a smiling conductor held the train until she jumped aboard. According to a friend, Eleanor thought it "odd that a great, tall woman like herself, who towered over everybody in Grand Central Station, would be recognized when she ran for a train and that they would hold the train for her. It

Mrs. Roosevelt christens the cabin plane "The Governor" at the Albany airport. Afterward, she boarded the plane and was flown over the state capital.

never occurred to her to ask to have the train held for the governor's lady."

Governor Roosevelt sought his wife's advice. He encouraged her to attend Democratic Party functions around the state as his representative. And he asked Eleanor to go with him when he made inspection tours of hospitals, asylums, and prisons. The governor would be driven around the grounds by the director of an institution. But because it was difficult for him to walk, he would send his wife into the buildings to act as his "eyes and ears."

"At first my reports were highly unsatisfactory to him," Eleanor recalled. "I would tell him what was on the menu for the day and he would ask: 'Did you look to see whether the inmates were actually getting that food?' I learned to look into the cooking pots on the stove to find out if the contents corresponded to the menu. I learned to notice whether the beds were too close together, and . . . to watch the patients' attitude toward the staff, and before the end of our years in Albany, I had become a fairly expert reporter on state institutions."

Eleanor Roosevelt became known as a First Lady who cared about people's problems and tried to help. She was swamped with letters. Aided by a secretary, she answered them herself or referred them to the appropriate state agency, asking to be informed of the action taken. Often, she would send a letter to her husband with a penciled note, "How shall I answer or will you?"

A woman whose son was in jail wrote several letters to the First Lady. "When she found out I could not help free him," Eleanor recalled, "she begged that I go see him, which I did. Now she begs that I go weekly . . . !"

During her personal travels around the state, Mrs. Roosevelt refused to ride in an official limousine. She wanted to drive herself, in her own car. Worried about her safety, Franklin assigned a strapping young state trooper named Earl Miller to act as the First Lady's guide and bodyguard. Earl was a former circus acrobat, an amateur boxing champ, a skilled horseman who did trick riding at the state fair, and a crack shot. His fellow troopers teased him about his new assignment, but he soon became one of

Assigned to accompany Mrs. Roosevelt as her bodyguard, state trooper Earl Miller became a lifelong friend.

Eleanor's admirers. He persuaded her to take up riding again, looked after her horse, coached her at tennis, and told her the story of his life. She welcomed him into her charmed circle of devoted friends.

"He gave something to Eleanor," said Marion Dickerman. "You know it was a very deep attachment. . . . It was very, very deep."

Eleanor and Earl spent so much time together that tongues wagged. They both laughed at the gossip. Earl had a busy and complicated romantic life. He married and divorced a number of times. But that did not affect his friendship with Eleanor or her lasting affection for him.

With the Roosevelts in residence, the ornate governor's mansion in Albany was a lively and informal meeting place. People were constantly coming and going, day and night. The Roosevelt boys brought their classmates to the statehouse from boarding school and college. Anna, now married, left her baby and her German shepherd with Eleanor and Franklin when she traveled with her husband. Dogs chased each other through the hallways. Books and magazines were strewn about everywhere. Large, talkative groups sat around the dinner table almost every evening.

Eleanor and Franklin shared an active political partnership and a mutual concern for their children, but their personal lives were separate in many ways. Franklin spent long periods at Warm Springs. Eleanor went there rarely. She was involved in her teaching, writing, and lecturing, and in running the Val-Kill furniture factory with Marion and Nan. She still spent the night in the big house at Hyde Park whenever her husband or her children were there, or when Franklin had important guests. But the stone cottage on the bank of Val-Kill Creek that she shared with Marion and Nan was her real home.

The swimming pool at Val-Kill. From the left: Eleanor, Franklin, Marguerite LeHand, and Earl Miller. Eleanor learned to swim so she could teach her younger boys.

While the Roosevelts led independent lives, they were also close. They looked to others for the warmth and intimacy of friendship, and yet they needed each other. One winter, Franklin wanted Eleanor to join him at Warm Springs, but he would not ask her directly. Instead, he wrote to Anna and told her how much he wanted to see Eleanor. Anna in turn wrote to her mother, saying that Franklin was worried that Eleanor was working too hard. He hoped she could get away to spend a week in Georgia with him. "If you think it would give you any rest at all to go to Warm Springs—do go," Anna wrote. "Pa seems to want you there so badly."

Later that year, Franklin's mother was vacationing in Paris when she fell ill with pneumonia. Franklin immediately sailed for Europe to fetch his mother and bring her back to New York. "I hated to see you go, though I knew it was the best thing for you to do & the sensible thing for me not to go," Eleanor wrote to her husband. "We are really very dependent on each other though we do see so little of each other. . . . Goodnight, dear. . . . I miss you & hate to feel you so far away."

During Franklin Roosevelt's first term as governor of New York, the United States went from boom to bust almost overnight. In October 1929, a sudden stock market crash sent the nation's economy into shock. Millions of people lost their jobs, factories closed, businesses failed. America faced the worst economic calamity in its history. As governor of an important industrial state, Roosevelt gained national attention by taking bold emergency measures to provide jobs for the unemployed and relief for the needy.

In 1930 he was reelected governor by the biggest margin ever recorded in New York State. His landslide victory immediately made him a front-runner for the presidential nomination in 1932.

Eleanor shared her husband's belief in a caring government that would act to aid the needy and unemployed, but she did not relish the idea of moving to the White House. In Albany she was still able to strike a balance between her personal interests and her duties as the governor's wife. It would be difficult to manage that in Washington, where the First Lady lived in the glare of national publicity.

Desperate for work, an unemployed man in Detroit advertises on a street corner.

People everywhere were homeless, hungry, and out of work.

When word came from Chicago that the Democratic National Convention had nominated Franklin Delano Roosevelt as the party's candidate for president in 1932, Eleanor joined in the midnight celebration at the governor's mansion in Albany. Friends, relatives, and aides cheered and embraced one another and gathered around the beaming governor for toasts of congratulations. While rejoicing for Franklin, Eleanor silently despaired for herself:

"I was happy for my husband, because I knew that in many ways it would make up for the blow that fate had dealt him when he was stricken with infantile paralysis; and I had implicit confidence in his ability to help the country in a crisis. . . .

"But for myself I was deeply troubled. As I saw it, this meant the end of any personal life of my own. I knew what traditionally should lie before me; I had watched Mrs. Theodore Roosevelt and had seen what it meant to be the wife of a president, and I cannot say that I was pleased at the prospect. . . . The turmoil in my heart and mind was rather great that night, and the next few months were not to make any clearer what the road ahead would be."

As expected, Eleanor became fully involved in the presidential campaign. She flew with Franklin to Chicago, where he accepted the nomination (it was the first plane trip ever made by a presidential candidate). Behind the scenes she helped plan and direct the activities of the women's division of the Democratic Party. And she traveled with Franklin on his campaign train. A reporter described her as "Gracious, charming, patient, serene . . . and plainly the devoted helpmate." The public could not have guessed that Eleanor Roosevelt dreaded going to the White House.

One of the reporters aboard the campaign train was Lorena Hickok of The Associated Press, a robust woman with mischievous eyes and a laugh that could cheer up a room. Hickok—or "Hick" as she came to be called—was impressed by Eleanor's warmth and kindness. And yet, she

Lorena Hickok, The Associated Press's highest-paid woman reporter.

*Reporters surround the future First Lady after FDR's presidential victory is assured,
November 8, 1932.*

sensed that Mrs. Roosevelt was deeply unhappy. As the two women became friends, Hick began to draw Eleanor out. Formal interviews gave way to spontaneous conversations and finally, to intimate heart-to-heart talks as Eleanor confided her anxieties and fears.

On election day, Franklin Roosevelt overwhelmingly defeated his Republican opponent, President Herbert Hoover. That night, as Eleanor faced the glare of newsreel lights and a mob of reporters, she did her best to smile. She seemed calm and detached, but Hick noticed a "miserable" expression in Eleanor's eyes. She thought that her friend looked like "a fox, surrounded by a pack of baying hounds."

A few days later, Eleanor was riding the train to Albany with Hick, returning from her classes at Todhunter School. "There isn't going to be any First Lady," she told the reporter. "There is just going to be plain, ordinary Mrs. Roosevelt. And that's all."

Even so, Eleanor knew that she would have to make major changes in her life. For one thing, as the president's wife she would have to give up teaching at Todhunter. "I've liked teaching more than anything else I've ever done," she said, "but it's got to go."

Then, as the train sped along the Hudson River on its way to Albany, Eleanor Roosevelt opened her bulging briefcase. She pulled out a folder filled with student papers and began to read them. "A teacher also has homework to do," she told Hick.

FDR with Eleanor and James after the inauguration, March 4, 1933.

✦ EIGHT ✦

A President's Wife

*"I never wanted to be a president's wife, and I don't
want it now. . . . Now I shall have to work out
my own salvation."*

An expectant, windswept crowd of one hundred thousand had gathered in front of the capitol under gray skies to watch Franklin Delano Roosevelt take his oath as the nation's thirty-second president. Eleanor Roosevelt—wearing a blue coat and a bouquet of white orchids—stood among eighty dark-suited men on the inaugural platform. She listened intently as her husband spoke.

On that raw winter day—March 4, 1933—the Great Depression was in its fourth destructive year. As many as fifteen million men and women—one-third of the available work force—had lost their jobs and could not find work. Thousands of banks had failed, wiping out the savings of their depositors. In America's great cities, hungry and homeless people stood in long lines at charity soup kitchens and foraged for food in garbage cans. Not since 1861, when Abraham Lincoln assumed leadership of a divided nation, had a new president faced such a crisis.

"This nation asks for action, and action now," Roosevelt declared. "I shall ask Congress for . . . broad Executive power to wage a war against the emergency, as great as the power that would be given to me if we were in fact invaded by a foreign foe."

Back at the White House, Lorena Hickok waited in the room that had

once been Abraham Lincoln's bedroom and would now be Eleanor
Roosevelt's sitting room and study. During the presidential campaign, the
two women had formed a close bond of friendship and mutual affection.
Hick knew better than anyone Eleanor's private anguish as she faced the
prospect of life in the White House.

Eleanor had promised her friend an exclusive interview following the
inauguration. "It was very, very solemn and a little terrifying," she told
Hick. "The crowds were so tremendous, and you felt that they would do
anything—if only someone would tell them *what* to do."

As he had promised, President Roosevelt acted swiftly to meet the crisis
and restore confidence. During his first hundred days in office he pushed
through Congress the most far-reaching legislative program in American
history. At the same time, Eleanor Roosevelt proved to herself and to an
astonished nation of Roosevelt watchers that she did not intend to be a
conventional White House hostess.

She broke with tradition when she announced that she would hold
regular press conferences open to women reporters only—an idea suggested
by Lorena Hickok. They would be the first press conferences ever given by
a First Lady, on the record, in the White House. Other presidential wives,
shielded from the press, had refused even to grant interviews. Eleanor
believed that the nation's citizens had a right to know what the people in
the White House were thinking and doing. She met with thirty-five "press
girls" for the first time on March 6, just two days after FDR's inauguration.

The White House staff was flabbergasted by the First Lady's easy
informality. In her eagerness to get settled, Eleanor pitched in and helped
move furniture around. She insisted on running the little wood-paneled
elevator herself, without waiting for a porter to run it for her. And she
refused to be shadowed by Secret Service agents whenever she went out.
"No one's going to hurt me," she said. "I simply can't imagine being afraid
of going among [Americans] as I always have, as I always shall."

Rather than go everywhere in a limousine, she bought a light-blue
Plymouth roadster—a sporty convertible with a rumble seat. She would
drive it herself, she announced, as she was accustomed to doing—without
a chauffeur or police escort. That summer, she invited Hick to join her on

Mrs. Roosevelt's White House press conferences gave women journalists a unique opportunity to report on political issues.

a three-week motor tour of New England and Canada. Eleanor had not yet been photographed often enough to be recognized. The two friends traveled as "ordinary tourists" without anyone realizing who they were.

Early in her husband's administration, Mrs. Roosevelt made a surprise appearance that dramatized her resolve to stay in touch with ordinary citizens. The year before, when Herbert Hoover was still president, thousands of unemployed war veterans had marched on Washington, demanding that bonuses promised them in the future be paid immediately. Hoover was so alarmed that he called out the Army. Troops commanded by General Douglas MacArthur routed the jobless veterans with tear gas and burned their encampment.

Shortly after FDR took office, the bonus marchers returned to the capital. This time the government opened an old army camp to house the men and provided them with food and medical care. Even so, many people feared that violence would erupt again. Critics charged that the unemployed veterans were led by Communist agitators who wanted to stir up trouble.

One afternoon, Eleanor took Louis Howe for a drive in her new roadster. He suggested that they stop by the veterans' encampment. When they arrived, he announced that he was going to sit in the car and wait while Eleanor toured the rows of tents. "Hesitatingly, I got out and walked over to where I saw a line-up of men waiting for food," she wrote later. "They looked at me curiously and one of them asked my name and what I wanted. When I said I just wanted to see how they were getting on, they asked me to join them."

Eleanor spent an hour chatting with the men. Before leaving, she joined in as everyone sang "There's a Long, Long Trail." "Then I got into the car and drove away," she recalled. "Everyone waved and I called, 'Good luck,' and they answered, 'Good-bye and good luck to you.'"

At her next press conference, Mrs. Roosevelt described the camp as "remarkably clean and orderly" and the veterans as "grand-looking boys with a fine spirit." Her unannounced visit and courteous reception helped calm the public's fears about the bonus marchers and created sympathy for their demands. She had discovered that a personal appearance by the First Lady could have a powerful impact on public opinion. As one of the veterans remarked: "Hoover sent the Army. Roosevelt sent his wife."

Never before had the American people seen a First Lady like Eleanor Roosevelt. Soon she was flying off all over the country, serving as her husband's personal investigative reporter and gathering material for her columns, articles, radio talks, and books. Reporters who covered the White House and traveled with Mrs. Roosevelt marveled at her energy and pace.

She was a frequent flier at a time when a trip in an airplane was considered a great adventure. Once, in order to impress the public with the ease and safety of air travel, Amelia Earhart invited the First Lady to join her on a flight from Washington to Baltimore. They both wore evening dresses. "How do you feel being piloted by a woman?" Eleanor was asked. "Absolutely safe," she replied. "I'd give a lot to do it myself!"

The first president's wife to fly, she earned the nickname "Eleanor Everywhere."

Eleanor seemed to go everywhere. Since she could travel more freely than Franklin, she again became his "eyes and ears." She dropped in on coal miners in Appalachia, slum-dwellers in Puerto Rico, and sharecroppers in their tarpaper shacks in southern cotton fields. And she inspected government relief projects from one end of the country to the other, "often managing to arrive without advance notice so that they could not be polished up for my inspection." Her sympathetic visits created a feeling among millions of Americans that someone in the highest levels of government cared about their problems.

She had been writing for newspapers and magazines since the 1920s. As First Lady, she began a daily syndicated newspaper column called "My Day," which reported on her travels and her life in the White House. She also wrote a monthly column, and turned out a steady flow of articles for magazines. And she wrote every word herself.

*A newspaper car-
toon salutes the First
Lady's far-flung
travels. "My Day"
appeared six times a
week in some 180
newspapers.*

My Day

By

ELEANOR ROOSEVELT

DES MOINES, Iowa, Monday.—A pleasant evening last night in
Chicago talking to Mr. and Mrs. Charles Braested and Louis Ruppel. I
reached the train a little before 11 o'clock and arrived here at 7:30 this
morning.

I cannot quite get accustomed to so much solicitude and attention on
the part of everybody. Some day I suppose I may expect to, but it
is still a surprise to me.

When I was called up last night and told I could not possibly travel

When critics complained that the First Lady's sentences were wordy and her topics trivial, magazine writer Bruce Bliven came to her defense: "I have a feeling that the New York sophisticates are all wrong and that the country as a whole likes the sort of person Mrs. Roosevelt has in her column demonstrated herself to be—friendly, unpretentious, possessed of inexhaustible vitality, a broad interest in all sorts of people and a human wish for their welfare."

Along with her writing, Eleanor spoke regularly on the radio and toured widely as a lecturer. She hired a voice coach who helped her modulate the high-pitched tones that sometimes marred her talks. When she rose to speak, she prayed silently that she would have something meaningful to say to the people in front of her. Then she focused on two or three faces in the audience. By speaking directly to those people, she was able to infuse her talk with warmth and spontaneity. She became one of the most popular lecturers in America.

She was admired for the calm and authoritative manner with which she handled questions after a speech, including those meant to embarrass her.

Speaking at the Chicago World's Fair, November 1, 1933.

One hostile questioner asked: "Do you think your husband's illness has affected his mentality?" Without changing her expression, Eleanor replied: "I am glad that question was asked. The answer is Yes. Anyone who has gone through great suffering is bound to have a greater sympathy and understanding of the problems of mankind." The audience gave her a standing ovation.

Mrs. Roosevelt used her lectures, her radio talks, her columns and articles, her press conferences, and her endless travels through America to publicize her views on social justice, and to help bring the White House closer to the American people. The most outspoken of First Ladies, she became a powerful advocate for the weak and disadvantaged in American society—for blacks and other minorities, for tenant farmers, the unemployed, the hungry and the homeless, for all those who had no platform or spokesperson of their own.

All sorts of people wrote to her appealing for help. During her first year in the White House she received more than three hundred thousand letters. "I have read and heard so many nice things about you, it's almost like writing to a friend," said one correspondent.

Among the many who wrote simply to wish Eleanor well was a young woman named Bertha Brodsky, who apologized for her handwriting. She found it difficult to write because her back was crooked. She had to walk "bent sideways," she added. Eleanor replied with an encouraging letter. She arranged for a specialist to examine Bertha and for the surgery that followed. Later she visited Bertha in the hospital, helped her find a job when she recovered, attended her wedding, and became godmother to her child.

While it was not humanly possible for her to answer every letter personally, each letter did receive a reply. Pleas for employment and complaints about government administrators were forwarded to the appropriate agency with a cover letter signed by the First Lady. One official recalled: "She looked at the thing and decided whose business it was in the government to find out about it and sent that letter with her own initials on it and wrote, 'Find out about this letter. You know what it's all about.' You'd better do it. She never forgot."

Wearing a miner's cap, Mrs. Roosevelt starts a two-and-a-half-mile trip down into an Ohio coal mine, May 21, 1935.

Eleanor Roosevelt's first book, a collection of articles and speeches titled *It's Up to the Women,* was published in 1933. It was a clarion call for women to take an active and progressive role in the nation's affairs.

The First Lady worked closely with Molly Dewson, head of the women's division of the Democratic National Committee. They were determined that women's voices be heard at every level of the new administration. And for the first time, women received more than token recognition. Frances Perkins, FDR's secretary of labor, was the first woman ever chosen to serve in a president's cabinet. Florence Allen became the first woman judge of the U.S. Court of Appeals. By the end of Roosevelt's first term, far more women than ever before held responsible government posts.

Eleanor played down her influence on these appointments. But she admitted that she would sometimes "go to my husband to say that I was very weary of reminding him to remind the members of his Cabinet and his advisers that women were in existence, that they were a factor in the life of the nation. . . . As a result, I was sometimes asked for suggestions and would mention two or three names."

During the depression, more than two million women were unemployed at a time when many jobs were reserved for men only. Mrs. Roosevelt organized a White House conference to gain support for programs that could aid jobless women. Through Eleanor's efforts, women's work relief projects became an important part of federal efforts to ease hardship and get the economy moving again.

Critics charged that the massive government relief programs of FDR's "New Deal" were wasteful or corrupt or socialistic. Mrs. Roosevelt disagreed. She welcomed this new direction in American public policy— the first time that the federal government had attempted to aid those citizens who suffered economic hardship through no fault of their own.

President Roosevelt had seized on the word *liberal* to describe his economic and social programs. New Deal liberalism, he said, "is plain English for a changed concept of the duty and responsibility of government toward economic life." During the 1930s, liberalism came to mean using government action to expand the choices available to the poor and the powerless.

Down and out on a San Francisco bread line.

Eleanor Roosevelt believed that an enlightened and caring government could bring about a more humane and just society. "The big achievement of the past two years is the great change in the thinking of the country," she told a press conference in 1935. "Imperceptibly we have come to recognize that government has a responsibility to defend the weak."

The First Lady took a special interest in government programs for the nation's youth. She worried about the effects of the depression on the lives of millions of young people who could not find jobs when they left school. "I have moments of real terror when I think we might be losing this generation," she said. She pressed government leaders to set up a special agency for young Americans. And she made a special appeal to her husband, who needed little prodding. In 1935, FDR signed an executive order creating the National Youth Administration (NYA). This agency provided grants to help high school and college students stay in school, and offered vocational training for unemployed youth.

The NYA was one of the most popular New Deal programs, but it still had its share of critics. Opponents charged that the agency undermined the initiative and self-reliance of the nation's youth. Segregationists objected to the NYA because black youngsters were included in its programs.

Discrimination against black Americans was widely accepted during the 1930s. In many parts of the country, including the nation's capital, blacks were barred from schools, restaurants, and hotels. Even movie theaters were segregated. Throughout the South, most blacks were not permitted to vote.

Like many white Americans of her social class and generation, Eleanor Roosevelt had grown up among people who rarely questioned racial and religious prejudices. Until she entered the White House, virtually all the blacks she had met were servants. As First Lady during a time of economic deprivation and suffering, she began to understand how deeply racial discrimination was embedded in American life.

Mrs. Roosevelt became an outspoken champion of civil rights. She visited black communities and schools, befriended black leaders, and learned at firsthand about the indignities and humiliations endured by blacks. Her racial views upset some of her husband's advisers. They feared that she was too radical, that "I might hurt my husband politically and socially."

FDR did not attempt to restrain his wife. He sympathized with Eleanor's ideals of social justice, but he preferred to let her take the lead. That way, he could gain political allies in the black community without losing the support of powerful southern segregationists, who controlled so many important committees in Congress. In any case, Franklin knew his wife too well to try to talk her out of any cause she wholeheartedly embraced.

The First Lady and Lorena Hickok visit a Puerto Rican slum.

More than any other public figure during the 1930s, Eleanor Roosevelt conveyed a message in word and deed that the federal government cared about racial justice. She believed that democracy could not fully be realized in America until both poverty and prejudice were conquered. "We have poverty which enslaves and racial prejudice which does the same," she said.

In 1939, Eleanor attended a meeting of the Southern Conference for Human Welfare in Birmingham, Alabama. When she arrived at the auditorium with black educator Mary McLeod Bethune, she was told that blacks and whites were not allowed to sit together at public gatherings in Birmingham. They were required by law to sit on opposite sides of an auditorium's center aisle. The First Lady refused to obey the segregation order. When the police told her that she was violating the law, she had a chair placed in the center aisle and sat there.

A few weeks later, people all over the world were shocked when the Daughters of the American Revolution (DAR) denied the use of its Washington, D.C., auditorium, Constitution Hall, for a concert by the celebrated black singer Marian Anderson. Three years earlier, Miss Anderson had been invited to sing at the White House. In 1939, however, the president of the DAR declared that no black artist would be permitted to appear in Constitution Hall—the only auditorium in Washington big enough to hold Miss Anderson's fans.

Mrs. Roosevelt was proud of her ancestors who had taken part in the Revolutionary War, but she decided that she could not remain a member of an organization that practiced blatant racism. She resigned from the DAR in protest, focusing worldwide attention on the episode.

Afterward, the Department of the Interior scheduled a free open-air concert on the steps of the Lincoln Memorial. More than seventy-five thousand people gathered on the mall in front of the monument that Sunday to hear the magnificent voice of contralto Anderson. Her opening number was "America," and she ended the concert with "Nobody Knows the Troubles I've Seen." "When I sang that day," Marian Anderson wrote later, "I was singing to the entire Nation."

Because Eleanor Roosevelt never hesitated to take a stand, she made

With educator Mary McLeod Bethune at a Washington conference organized by the National Youth Administration.

enemies as well as friends. Her critics were offended by her liberal views, her highly publicized travels, and her spirited independence. They called her a meddlesome busybody, a do-gooder, a woman who did not know her place. "I wish that Mrs. Roosevelt would stick to her knitting and keep out of the affairs connected with my department," complained Interior Secretary Harold Ickes.

Eleanor replied that she was sorry if her activities offended anyone, but she was determined to pursue her interests and express her beliefs. "Everyone must live their own life in their own way and not according to anybody else's ideas," she told a press conference.

Since she advocated social reforms that went far beyond the proposals of the New Deal, Eleanor was often branded a "socialist" or a "communist." But the most savage attacks came from those who were enraged that the First Lady of the land would speak out against segregation and discrimination. They spread nasty rumors about her personal habits and social life. And they warned that her views on civil rights would ignite violent confrontations between whites and blacks.

Eleanor's admirers saw her as an inspirational figure, a woman of compassion who listened with sympathy and understanding to the con-

Anna, Eleanor, and Sara listen to FDR accept the Democratic nomination in 1936.

cerns of ordinary people. They marveled at her energy, her honesty, and her independent stance as a woman making a mark on the world. For many American parents during the Great Depression, naming a child "Eleanor" was like bestowing the name of a saint.

When FDR ran for his second term in 1936, Eleanor joined her husband aboard his campaign train. At every stop, jubilant crowds who gathered to cheer the president demanded a glimpse of the First Lady, too. "If she failed to appear on the platform, they shouted for her until she did appear, and they cheered her just as heartily as her husband, sometimes more heartily," a reporter wrote.

FDR won a resounding victory that year. He defeated his Republican opponent, Alfred M. Landon of Kansas, by nearly eleven million votes—the biggest popular plurality ever recorded in an American election.

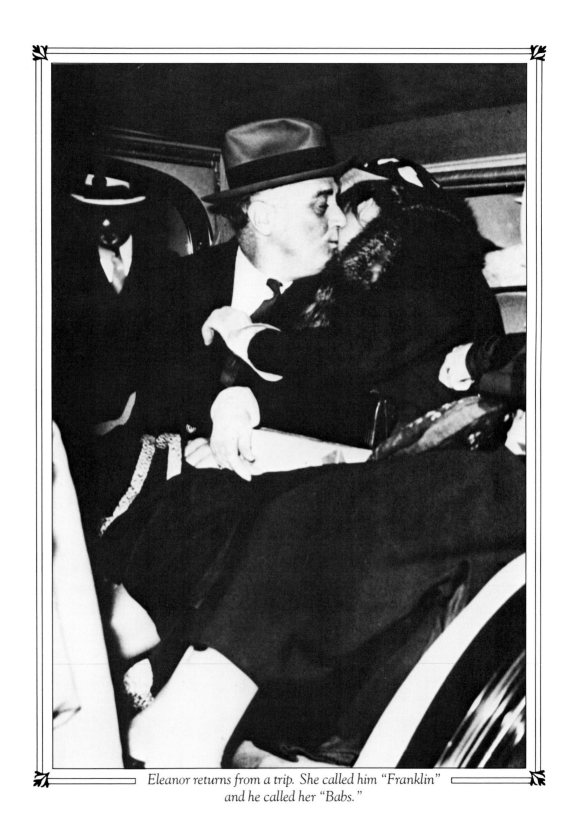

Eleanor returns from a trip. She called him "Franklin"
and he called her "Babs."

✦ NINE ✦

Partners

"I'm the agitator; he's the politician."

Throughout their presidential years, Eleanor and Franklin observed a ritual. Whenever Eleanor returned from a trip, she would dine informally with Franklin that evening so she could report to him while her impressions were still fresh. He always questioned her closely. Because his questions covered such a wide range, "I became, as the years went by, a better reporter and a better observer," she wrote. "I found myself obliged to notice everything."

The president often used his wife as a sounding board. When they discussed a controversial issue, he would bait Eleanor by taking a stand he knew she would oppose. Then he would listen carefully to her arguments. Sometimes he surprised her by changing his mind and adopting her point of view. "If I felt strongly about anything, I told him," she wrote, "since he had the power to do things and I did not, but he did not always feel as I did."

Economist Rexford Tugwell, a member of FDR's "Brain Trust," witnessed many discussions between the president and the first lady. He wrote: "No one who ever saw Eleanor Roosevelt sit down facing her husband, and, holding his eyes firmly, say to him, 'Franklin, I think you should . . .' or, 'Franklin, surely you will not . . .' will ever forget the experience."

Eleanor had many ways of calling Franklin's attention to issues and causes she felt were important. She invited all sorts of people to the White House. At dinner, she arranged the seating so that FDR would find himself in conversation with the author of a book she wanted him to read, or the representative of a group whose cause she favored. "I'm the agitator; he's the politician," she said. Others called her the "conscience" of the New Deal. "In a way, my conscience bothered him," she admitted. "And that's [a] perfectly natural thing. He was a very human person in a great many ways."

Although FDR listened to his wife, he was keenly attuned to what he believed was politically possible. If he felt that Eleanor threatened to stir up more public controversy than he was willing to tolerate, he would ask her to pull back. She understood that as First Lady, there were limits to what she could say or do. "While I often felt strongly on various subjects, Franklin frequently refrained from supporting causes he believed in because of political realities," she wrote.

One of their sharpest disagreements concerned America's participation in the World Court, which had been set up after World War I to help settle disputes among nations. Eleanor had worked hard and long to promote American entry into the Court. Opponents of the Court argued that the United States should not be involved in international organizations. The issue was so controversial that Franklin tried to avoid it during his campaign for president in 1932. Refusing to take sides, he withdrew his earlier support for both the World Court and the League of Nations.

Eleanor was furious. When Franklin saw how upset she was, he invited her good friend Agnes Leach, head of the League of Women Voters, to lunch. "Eleanor is very fond of you," he explained, "and you can make peace between us. She hasn't spoken to me in three days."

But Agnes Leach, like Eleanor, was a dedicated internationalist and peace advocate. She turned down Franklin's invitation. "That was a shabby statement [about the World Court]," she told him. "I just don't feel like having lunch with you today."

Afterward, Eleanor phoned her friend and said, "Agnes, you are a sweet, darling girl. I hear you upset Franklin very much. I didn't know you had it in you."

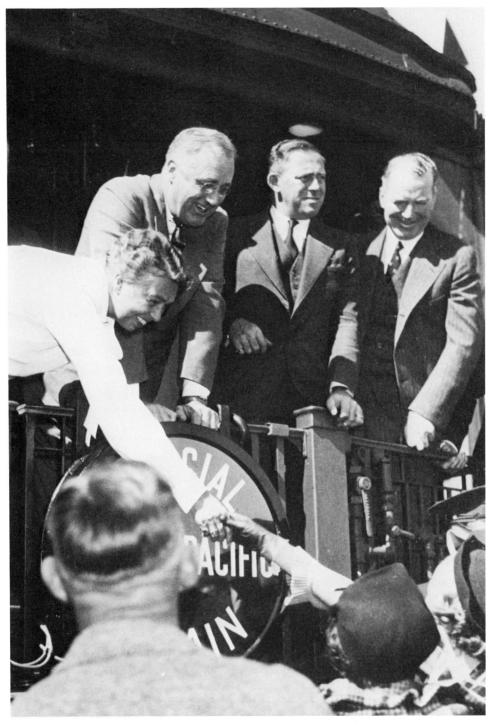

The president and Mrs. Roosevelt stop at Fremont, Nebraska, during a western train tour, September 1935.

Civil rights legislation was another issue that caused friction between Eleanor and Franklin. The first lady fought for civil rights in the early days of the New Deal when that term was not even known. She was one of the few in Washington ready to do so. Time and again she urged her husband to support laws banning discrimination, even when he was not ready to take action, when his advisors were worried about a white backlash. Some of his aides felt that Mrs. Roosevelt was dangerously idealistic.

Franklin respected his wife's ideals. "You go right ahead and stand for whatever you feel is right," he told her. ". . . I have to stand on my own legs. Besides, I can always say that I can't do a thing with you."

FDR's hands-off policy had advantages for both of them. It meant that Eleanor's outspoken opinions could serve as trial balloons: "If some idea I expressed strongly—and with which he might agree—caused a violent reaction, he could honestly say that he had no responsibility in the matter and that the thoughts were my own."

At the end of FDR's second term, political commentator Raymond Clapper included Eleanor Roosevelt in his list of "The Ten Most Powerful People in Washington." He called her "a force on public opinion, on the President, and on the government . . . the most influential woman of our times."

In the White House living quarters, the president and the First Lady each had their own private suites. And they were each surrounded by their own circle of loyal friends and aides. When guests arrived at the executive mansion for dinner, they often had cocktails with Eleanor or with Franklin in their separate suites before everyone came together in the dining room.

Over the years, a surprising number of friends and aides lived at the White House as members of the Roosevelts' extended family. Louis Howe, who was close to both Eleanor and Franklin, occupied a suite across the hall from Eleanor's quarters until his death in 1936. Marguerite "Missy" LeHand, FDR's devoted personal assistant, had joined the Roosevelt household in Albany and moved with them to Washington. She accompanied the president on many of his trips and acted as White House hostess when Eleanor was away.

Lorena Hickok also stayed at the White House during much of the late 1930s, living in the bedroom once occupied by Louis Howe. Hick had resigned from The Associated Press, fearing that her friendship with the First Lady compromised her objectivity. She traveled widely around the country, writing eloquent reports on the human costs of the depression for federal relief agencies. Eleanor continued to confide in her. When Hick was away, the two friends wrote to each other nearly every day.

The remaining White House guest rooms were usually filled with friends and visiting dignitaries, with the Roosevelt children, their spouses, and a growing brood of grandchildren. When Anna separated from her husband, she and her two small children moved into the executive mansion. James also lived there for a time with his wife and little girl. There were nurseries on the third floor and a jungle gym on the south lawn. Franklin, Jr., and John brought their friends home from Harvard. The housekeeper was instructed to keep the icebox full for midnight snacks. "It was like visiting friends in a very large country house," said one White House guest.

Informal family dinners were noisy and spirited, "with all of them talking at one and the same time," according to Harold Ickes, who described a dinner he attended: "Mrs. Roosevelt . . . [raised] some social question and her three sons at once began to wave their arms in the air and take issue with her. . . . The President joined in at intervals, but he wasn't President of the United States on that occasion—he was merely the father of three sons who had opinions of their own. They interrupted him when they felt like it and all talked at him at the same time. It was really most amusing."

Inside the family and out, there were plenty of jokes about Eleanor's far-flung travels. It was said that Admiral Richard Byrd always set two places for supper at his solitary South Pole hut, just in case Mrs. Roosevelt should drop in. And yet much of Eleanor's traveling was done to keep in touch with her grown children and their families as they scattered across the country. She would visit to celebrate a birthday, to inspect a new grandchild, to nurse someone through an illness, to offer comfort and advice.

She was still the one the family turned to in times of trouble. Franklin

On the White House lawn with her grandchildren "Sistie" and "Buzzie" Dall, Anna's girl and boy.

Eleanor loved picnics. Here she cooks franks over an open fire at an outing for naval officers on Campobello Island.

was tied down by his presidential duties, and, while he was deeply devoted to his children, he had never been comfortable discussing personal matters. "Father had great difficulty talking about anything purely personal or private," Franklin, Jr., recalled, "especially if it involved anything unpleasant. He left that to Mother."

The Roosevelt children had more than their share of divorces, scandals, and personal crises. As the children of public figures, they found it hard to lead private lives, and their missteps and mistakes often made headlines. Like most parents, Eleanor and Franklin loyally supported their children. They rallied to their defense when they were in trouble, but they tried not to interfere in their lives. "No one ever lives up to the best in themselves all the time," Eleanor once said, "and nearly all of us love people because of their weaknesses rather than because of their strengths."

Eleanor followed a strict schedule when she was in Washington. She was up early and either did exercises in her room or went riding in Rock Creek Park on her horse, Dot. Back at the White House, there were often guests for breakfast. FDR always had breakfast alone in his room, so he could read the morning newspapers without being disturbed. When Eleanor saw the breakfast tray going in to Franklin, she would slip into his room to say good morning and exchange a few words.

Riding in Rock Creek Park with Mrs. Henry Morgenthau, Jr.

At her desk in the White House with Malvina Thompson, her personal assistant, and Edith Helm (standing), her social secretary.

After breakfast, she went over the day's schedule with the chief usher of the White House, the social secretary, and the housekeeper. Then she settled down to work with her personal assistant, Malvina Thompson. Mrs. Roosevelt would dictate letters, work on a column, an article, or a radio talk, receive visitors, and make phone calls. A typical day might include a morning press conference, lunch for the wives of cabinet members, and an afternoon appearance at a benefit. Returning to the executive mansion, she would change into an evening dress in record time and welcome guests to a formal state dinner.

Late at night, after the last guests had left, there were always reports and manuscripts to read, and a pile of mail waiting to be answered. Still in evening dress, Eleanor would work in her study. She liked to be surrounded by photographs, and the walls of the room were covered with framed portraits of friends, family, and people she admired. Her desk stood by a tall window that overlooked a magnolia tree planted a century earlier by President Andrew Jackson.

A White House Christmas. Eleanor bought presents throughout the year and kept them in a special closet until Christmas day.

Before retiring, she would go into Franklin's room to say goodnight. Often it was the only time of the day that she could really be alone with him. She would sit on his bed and talk frankly about the things on her mind.

Her schedule was so busy that a free evening was a luxury, and a worthy subject for one of her newspaper columns. In 1936 she told readers of "My Day": "Yesterday I enjoyed that rare thing for me, an evening of leisure. I dined on a little table in front of my fireplace, read all the things my briefcase contained that I had been waiting for days to read, did some knitting that required a little bit of attention and could not be done automatically . . . and enjoyed the company of a friend."

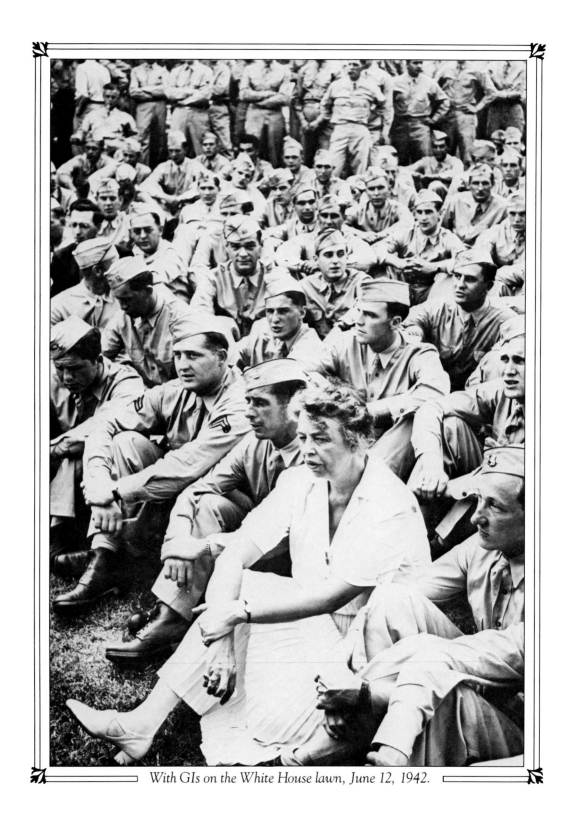

With GIs on the White House lawn, June 12, 1942.

TEN

The War Years

*"I imagine every mother felt as I did when I said
good-bye to [my sons] during the war. I had a feeling
that I might be saying good-bye for the last time."*

"At five o'clock this morning, our telephone rang," Eleanor Roosevelt reported from Hyde Park in "My Day" on September 2, 1939, "and it was the President in Washington to tell me the sad news that Germany had invaded Poland and that her planes were bombing Polish cities."

Adolf Hitler's troops had marched into Poland on September 1. Two days later, Britain and France declared war on Germany, launching the Second World War.

The First World War had ended just twenty-one years earlier, in 1918. Eleanor had never forgotten her visit with Franklin to Europe's battlefields, hospitals, and cemeteries. She had returned home with a deeply felt hatred of warfare that remained a ruling passion for the rest of her life. As First Lady during the 1930s, she made world peace one of her top priorities. She supported antiwar groups and appealed for worldwide disarmament in her columns, radio broadcasts, and lectures.

And yet hopes for peace were fading as totalitarian regimes grabbed power in Nazi Germany, Fascist Italy, and Imperial Japan. In 1937, Japanese warlords attacked China. In 1938, Hitler seized Austria, and in March 1939, Nazi troops took over Czechoslovakia. That same month, Fascist forces supported by Germany and Italy overthrew the democratic

Spanish republic, ending a civil war in Spain that had cost nearly a million lives.

Eleanor Roosevelt had described herself as "a very realistic pacifist." Now she was repelled by the brutal aggression taking place in Europe and Asia, and by the wanton bombing of cities and civilians in Spain and China. Although the United States maintained a policy of strict neutrality, she told her readers that "I am not neutral in feeling, as I believe in Democracy and the right of a people to choose their own government without having it imposed on them by Hitler and Mussolini."

As World War II approached, growing numbers of Jewish and other anti-Nazi refugees were clamoring for asylum in the United States. Eleanor threw all her influence behind a campaign to rescue some of these people. She wanted Congress to ease the nation's strict immigration laws and provide a safe haven for refugees trying to escape from Hitler.

With FDR's backing, the First Lady supported special legislation to admit ten thousand Jewish children a year for two years, over and above the regular immigration quota from Germany. A Quaker organization, the American Friends Service Committee, had enlisted all the families needed to guarantee homes for the children. And yet the Child Refugee Bill was denounced by isolationists and patriotic groups that wanted immigration to America restricted rather than liberalized. Finally the bill was withdrawn by its sponsors, who feared that existing immigration quotas might be *cut* by Congress rather than increased. The refugee children were never admitted.

"What has happened to us in this country?" Eleanor asked in her column. "If we study our own history we find that we have always been ready to receive the unfortunates from other countries, and though this may seem a generous gesture on our part, we have profited a thousandfold by what they have brought us."

With the outbreak of war, the refugees' plight became even more urgent. Thousands of desperate men, women, and children were begging for visas to the United States. In her public statements, and behind the scenes at the White House, Mrs. Roosevelt continued to plead the cause of Europe's refugees, but with little success. Only a handful of refugees

Nazi troops gather at Nuremberg.

Guarded by Nazi soldiers, Polish Jews from the Warsaw ghetto are marched off to death camps.

were able to overcome official barriers and find safety in the United States.

Protected by wide oceans on either shore, America watched from afar as Japan took over much of China and as Hitler's war machine conquered western Europe. In the summer of 1940, France surrendered. The Battle of Britain began as Nazi bombers roared across the English Channel day after day to rain bombs on London and other cities. The Roosevelt administration sent aid to Britain, increased military spending, and slowly prepared for war.

No American president had ever served more than two terms in office. But with the world gripped by crisis, FDR's supporters urged him to run for a third term. Mrs. Roosevelt told friends that she did not want to spend another four years in the White House. She felt that her husband had done his part, that he was ready to retire to Hyde Park and assume the role of elder statesman. "I had every evidence to believe that he did not want to run again," she wrote. "However, as time went on, more and more people came to me saying that he must run, that the threat of war was just over the horizon and no one else had the prestige and the knowledge to carry on through a crisis."

When the Democrats held their national convention in Chicago in 1940, FDR won renomination on the first ballot. During the presidential campaign that fall, his Republican opponent, Wendell Willkie, charged that Roosevelt would lead America into war. FDR countered by assuring "mothers and fathers [that] your boys are not going to be sent into any foreign wars. . . . The purpose of our defense is defense."

Mrs. Roosevelt was more cautious. "No one can honestly promise you today peace at home or abroad," she wrote in her column. "All any human being can do is to promise that he will do his utmost to prevent this country being involved in war."

The First Lady addresses the Democratic National Convention in Chicago, July 18, 1940.

Willkie's supporters tried to make the first lady herself a campaign issue. They distributed millions of buttons that said: WE DON'T WANT ELEANOR EITHER. "The campaign is as bad in personal bitterness as any I have ever been in," Eleanor told a friend. "I'll be glad when it is all over."

FDR won his third term easily, defeating Willkie by nearly five million votes. "As usual, I wanted him to win," wrote Eleanor, "since that was what he wanted, and I would have been sorry for his sake if he had been defeated."

The months following the election were a difficult time personally for Eleanor Roosevelt. In 1941, all four of her sons were called to active duty in the armed forces. She knew that if the United States actually entered the war, there was a good chance that not all of them would return safely.

All four Roosevelt sons served on active duty: Elliott in the air force, James in the marines, John and Franklin, Jr., in the navy.

Franklin's mother died that year at Hyde Park. A few weeks later, Eleanor lost her brother Hall, a victim, like their father, of alcoholism. Eleanor had loved Hall dearly, had worried about him all his life, and had "watched with great anxiety a fine mind gradually deteriorate." When he passed away, she could barely contain her grief.

She was thankful that she could immerse herself in a challenging new job. As the nation moved closer to war, she had wanted to play a useful role. FDR had created a new agency, the Office of Civilian Defense. He asked Eleanor to become its codirector with New York Mayor Fiorello LaGuardia.

The First Lady was working in her White House study on the afternoon of Sunday, December 7, 1941, when word came that Japanese planes had bombed Pearl Harbor. The next day, President Roosevelt asked Congress for a declaration of war. "I was deeply unhappy," Eleanor wrote. "I remembered my anxieties about my husband and brother when World War I began; now I had four sons of military age."

At the White House the next day, blackout curtains were placed on all the windows. Gun crews took up positions on the roof. A steam shovel went to work on the front lawn, digging a trench for a bomb shelter. Gas masks were distributed and air raid drills became a regular part of the White House routine.

Eleanor Roosevelt's job at the Office of Civilian Defense was the only official post she ever held in her husband's administration. Almost immediately, opponents of the New Deal began to denounce her policies and the people she appointed. As she had feared, she became a lightning rod for attacks by enemies of FDR, who dared not attack the president himself in wartime. Early in 1942, she decided to resign. "I realize how unwise it is for a vulnerable person like myself to try a government job," she admitted.

She had no intention of sitting out the war, however. FDR suggested that she accept an invitation from Queen Elizabeth to visit England and report on the contributions that British women were making to the war effort.

In the fall of 1942, Mrs. Roosevelt flew to England with her secretary, Malvina Thompson. For security reasons, their flight was kept secret. "Since Miss Thompson and I traveled under very unimaginative names and our bags looked like everyone else's, there was no easy method of identifying us," wrote Eleanor. "But, as I stepped out of the plane, I heard someone say, 'Why, there is Mrs. Roosevelt!' "

In London she saw the devastation caused by Nazi bombers. She talked with American paratroopers who would soon take part in the Allied

In bomb-ravaged London, October 1942.

invasion of North Africa. And she met British women who were working in war factories, serving as air traffic controllers, flying planes from one part of the country to another, and performing other "unfeminine" tasks—convincing Eleanor that American women could also play a useful role in the war effort. British journalists had to work in shifts to keep up with the energetic First Lady. "Hustle, did you say?" wrote one reporter. "She walked me off my feet!"

Like any other plane passenger at that time, Mrs. Roosevelt had been permitted only forty-four pounds of luggage for her three-week trip. Newspaper photos showed her wearing the same clothes time and again—a black wool coat, a blue-fox scarf, and a memorable cherry-red hat adorned with red and green birds' wings. She cheerfully called the outfit her "battle dress."

She was so successful as a goodwill ambassador that the president asked her to make other wartime trips. In 1943, the First Lady visited American troops in the South Pacific war zone. This time she left her secretary behind and traveled alone as a representative of the Red Cross. The portable typewriter on which she wrote her newspaper column was included among the forty-four pounds of luggage she was allowed to carry. She solved the weight problem by wearing simple Red Cross uniforms throughout the trip—a cool blue-gray jacket and skirt and a white blouse.

Eleanor turned fifty-nine that year. She traveled twenty-three thousand miles in a cramped, unheated, four-engined Army Liberator bomber equipped as a transport, visiting Australia, New Zealand, and seventeen South Pacific islands. At first, American military commanders in the region had grave misgivings about the First Lady's trip. The admirals and generals were unwilling to let Mrs. Roosevelt approach "danger spots" such as Guadalcanal in the Solomon Islands and Port Moresby off the coast of Australia.

Admiral William F. Halsey, chief of all naval operations in the Pacific, regarded Mrs. Roosevelt as a meddlesome "do-gooder" and "dreaded" her visit. But once he met her on the island of New Caledonia, and watched as she visited wounded servicemen, he began to sing her praises. She walked down endless hospital corridors, stepping into every ward, stopping at every bed, speaking to every patient as though he were her personal friend and only concern. At times she had to steel herself to keep from flinching at a wounded man's bedside. "I marveled at her hardihood, both physical and mental," Halsey wrote in his memoirs. "She walked for miles, and she saw patients who were grievously and gruesomely wounded. But I marveled most at their expressions as she leaned over them. It was a sight I will never forget."

On island after island, wherever the first lady appeared in her sturdy walking shoes and crisp Red Cross uniform, astonished soldiers would exclaim, "Gosh, there's Eleanor!" She awoke at reveille, went to breakfast with the enlisted men, rode with them in jeeps, comforted the wounded, and greeted the troops being trucked off to battle. After watching her maintain a schedule that would exhaust a drill sergeant, Admiral Halsey changed his mind and approved a stop at Guadalcanal. "I was ashamed of my original surliness," he confessed.

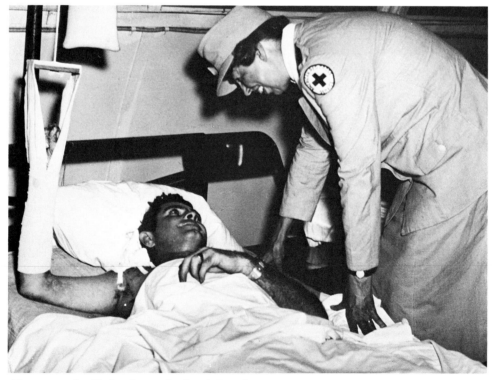

Greeting a disabled sailor in the South Pacific.

The crew of an aircraft carrier cheers Mrs. Roosevelt.

Guadalcanal had seen some of the bloodiest fighting of the war and was still being bombed by Japanese warplanes. During her stay on the island, Eleanor had a chance to visit a close personal friend, a young army sergeant named Joseph P. Lash. They had met in 1939, when Lash had just returned from fighting with the Loyalists in the Spanish Civil War. Eleanor had taken the idealistic young man under her wing. He became a trusted confidant and later, her dedicated biographer.

In a letter to his fiancée, Trude Pratt, Joseph Lash described "a very tired Mrs. Roosevelt, agonized by the men she had seen in the hospitals, fiercely determined because of them to be relentless in working for a peace that this time will last, a very loving and motherly Mrs. Roosevelt, and despite the heat, the weariness, and the tragedy, a gracious and magnificent lady."

During her grueling five-week trip, the First Lady lost thirty pounds. She arrived home so exhausted that friends worried about her health. Even she admitted that she felt weary. Unfriendly congressmen and newspapers were quick to criticize her trip as a political stunt. They ridiculed the First Lady as a persistent pest who flew all over the world at government expense. But to the four hundred thousand servicemen who saw Mrs. Roosevelt in camps and hospitals and rest centers, her trip was a resounding success. Admiral Halsey declared that "she alone had accomplished more good than any other person, or any group of civilians, who had passed through my area."

Eleanor Roosevelt never forgot the mutilation and misery she saw among wounded servicemen in the South Pacific. "If we don't make this a more decent world to live in I don't see how we can look these boys in the eyes," she told her friend Joseph Lash. "They are going to fight their handicaps all their lives & what for if the world is the same cruel, stupid place?"

Back in the White House she continued to press and prod her husband on behalf of issues she cared deeply about. But she had to tread more softly now than before. Weighed down by responsibilities, the president did not always welcome his wife's suggestions and pleas. He no longer had the stamina to debate issues with her.

At the U.S. Naval Hospital in San Diego, July 19, 1944.

As the war continued, the pressures of the presidency were wearing away at FDR's energy and health. Some of his aides felt that Mrs. Roosevelt failed to realize how weary the president was, and that he had to escape from his duties now and then. Eleanor knew that Franklin tired easily. She was concerned about his health. And yet her sense of responsibility and urgency drove her to keep after Franklin.

Among friends, Eleanor radiated warmth and sympathy. She could draw strangers to her and put them at ease. But she had never been good at the kind of lighthearted banter and dinner-table chitchat that could help the president forget his worries and relax. Their son James wrote that the one thing his mother could not provide "was that touch of triviality [Franklin] needed to ease his burden."

Eleanor was glad that their daughter was living in the White House while her second husband was overseas. Anna could offer the kind of easy, uncritical companionship that Franklin craved. She "brought to all her contacts a gaiety and buoyancy that made everybody feel happier because she was around," Eleanor wrote. Anna had taken over many of the duties that had once been handled by FDR's personal secretary, "Missy" LeHand, before her death. She helped her father in innumerable ways and served as White House hostess when Eleanor was away.

Despite the concern of friends and aides about the president's flagging health, there was never any doubt that he would run for a *fourth* term. As the 1944 election approached, Allied forces were advancing in Europe and across the Pacific. Victory was in sight. FDR wanted to be on hand to help establish a lasting peace. Doctors who examined him decided that if he would stop smoking and follow strict rules, he could continue his work.

Eleanor's hopes for the postwar world, and her confidence in her husband's leadership, overruled her worries about his health. "I dread another campaign and even more another four years in Washington, but since he's running for the good of the country I hope he wins," she said. FDR did win, defeating his Republican opponent, Thomas E. Dewey, by more than three and a half million votes—a tribute to Roosevelt's wartime leadership.

After his inaugural in January 1945, the president traveled by sea and air to the Russian city of Yalta for a Big Three summit meeting with British Prime Minister Winston Churchill and Soviet Premier Joseph Stalin. FDR returned to Washington looking haggard and frail. When he reported on the Yalta conference at a joint session of Congress, many senators and representatives were shocked at his appearance.

Soon afterward he left for a working vacation at Warm Springs, accompanied by two cousins, Laura Delano and Margaret Suckley. Eleanor was glad that Franklin would be able to enjoy their company. "I knew that they would not bother him as I should have by discussing questions of state," she confessed. "He would be allowed to get a real rest

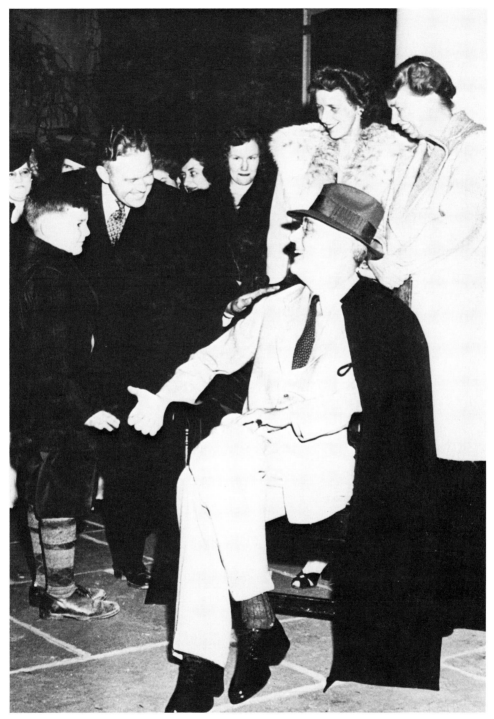

Election night at Hyde Park, November 7, 1944. FDR receives his neighbors on the porch of his home.

and yet would have companionship—and that was what I felt he most needed."

"Dearest Franklin," she wrote to him on the evening of April 8, "I haven't felt sleepy tonight so I've written James, Elliott, & Frankie, Elinor Morgenthau, Rommie & Sistie & now I must go to bed. . . .

"Give my love to Laura & Margaret & I'm glad they'll be along on the trip to San Francisco [to attend the founding session of the United Nations Organization with Eleanor and Franklin]. Much love to you dear. . . . You sounded cheerful for the first time last night & I hope you'll weigh 170 lbs when you return."

It was the last letter that Eleanor would send to her husband.

On the afternoon of April 12, 1945, Eleanor Roosevelt was attending a benefit when she was called to the phone. The president's press secretary, Steve Early, asked her to return to the White House right away. "I did not even ask why," she wrote. "I knew in my heart that something dreadful had happened."

When she arrived, she was told that her husband had suffered a massive cerebral hemorrhage at his Warm Springs cottage. The president had died at 3:35 that afternoon.

Eleanor sat silently for a few minutes. Then she turned to the somber duties that awaited her. She arranged to fly to Warm Springs that evening. And she sent for the vice-president, Harry S. Truman, asking him to come to the White House immediately. Truman had no idea why the invitation sounded so urgent.

A stunned Harry Truman learned from Eleanor Roosevelt that he was now the president of the United States. At first he could not bring himself to speak. Finally he asked: "Is there anything I can do for you?"

"Is there anything *we* can do for *you*?" Eleanor replied. "For you are the one in trouble now."

Her cable to her sons at their posts overseas read: PA SLIPPED AWAY THIS AFTERNOON. HE DID HIS JOB TO THE END AS HE WOULD WANT YOU TO DO.

When she arrived in Warm Springs late that night, she sat on a sofa in the living room of Franklin's cottage and asked his cousins to tell her exactly what had happened. Laura Delano described Franklin's last moments. He had been posing for a portrait artist just before lunch, and joking with his guests, when suddenly he put his hand to his head and collapsed. He never regained consciousness.

Eleanor listened quietly. Finally she rose from the sofa, walked to the bedroom where Franklin lay, and closed the door behind her. After five minutes, she emerged solemn and dry-eyed.

It was then that she asked about the portrait. Laura admitted that it had been commissioned by Franklin's old friend Lucy Mercer Rutherfurd, as a gift for Lucy's daughter. Lucy had married Winthrop Rutherfurd in 1920, shortly after her affair with Franklin. She was now a widow with grown children. She had visited Franklin at Warm Springs that day.

Eleanor learned for the first time that Franklin and Lucy Mercer had seen each other a number of times in recent years. When Eleanor was away, Lucy had been invited to dine at the White House along with other guests. Anna had served as hostess, feeling that it would do no harm if her father and Lucy revived a friendship that had meant so much to them both so long ago. It was all open and aboveboard—except that Eleanor was never told. She knew now.

The next day she boarded the funeral train that would carry Franklin Roosevelt back to Washington, and from there to his final resting place in the rose garden at Hyde Park. A military honor guard surrounded the flag-draped coffin in the last car of the train, where Franklin had sat so often. Eleanor lay in her berth with the window shade up, gazing out at the countryside her husband had loved, at the silent knots of people who gathered at every country crossroads to watch the train pass, at the weeping and sorrowful men and women who crowded every station platform along the way. And as the train moved northward across Georgia and the Carolinas and into the night, Eleanor Roosevelt was alone with her own bittersweet memories, and her grief.

At the simple funeral service in the White House, Mrs. Roosevelt wore a single piece of jewelry on her black widow's dress—the small golden pin shaped like a fleur-de-lis that her husband had given her as a wedding gift forty years before.

Mrs. Roosevelt follows her husband into the White House for the last time.

Eleanor once told a friend that she had not really been in love with Franklin since her discovery of his affair with Lucy Mercer. She had served Franklin willingly because she had faith in his leadership and shared his goals, but she was not in love with him. "There is no fundamental love to draw on, just respect and affection," she confided to Esther Lape.

"That is what she told me," Esther Lape said. "That was her story. Maybe she even half believed it. But I didn't. I don't think she ever stopped loving someone she loved."

When Eleanor wrote the second volume of her autobiography, *This I Remember,* she described her husband's death, but never mentioned Lucy Mercer Rutherfurd.

"Men and women who live together through long years get to know one another's failings," she wrote. "But they also come to know what is worthy of respect and admiration in those they live with and in themselves. . . .

"He might have been happier with a wife who was completely uncritical. That I was never able to be, and he had to find it in other people. Nevertheless, I think I sometimes acted as a spur, even though the spurring was not always wanted or welcome. I was one of those who served his purposes."

On May 7, 1945 — 25 days after FDR's death — Germany signed unconditional surrender terms. The next day, Mrs. Roosevelt broadcast a V-E (Victory in Europe) message to the American people.

"I am interested in every child who needs help,
and I am ready to help him."

ELEVEN

On Her Own

"Life has got to be lived—that's all there is to it."

"The story is over," Eleanor Roosevelt told a reporter shortly after her husband's death. With FDR gone, she doubted that she could play much of a role in the postwar world.

It was hard to accept Franklin's absence after a forty-year marriage. Writing to Joseph Lash she said, "I want to cling to those I love because I find that mentally I counted so much on Franklin I feel a bit bereft."

She was sixty years old and on her own. As she came to terms with her loss, she realized that the world was watching. The story was far from over. "I did not want to cease trying to be useful in some way," she wrote. "I did not want to feel old. . . ."

The new president came to Eleanor Roosevelt for advice. Harry Truman valued her insider's knowledge of Washington and was mindful of her influence. He wanted her on his side as he tried to fill FDR's gigantic shoes.

When Japan surrendered on August 14, 1945, ending World War II, Truman personally called Mrs. Roosevelt in Hyde Park to give her the news. Later he asked her to serve as one of five American delegates to the first meeting of the United Nations General Assembly, to be held in London that winter. Eleanor hesitated. She told the president that she had no real experience in foreign affairs and knew little about parliamentary procedure. But her friends urged her to accept, and finally she did, beginning "one of the most wonderful and worthwhile experiences in my life." She believed that the United Nations was FDR's most important legacy. Her appointment as a delegate was a tribute to him, she said.

The other American delegates were men: Secretary of State James F. Byrnes; Senator Tom Connally of Texas; Senator Arthur H. Vandenberg of Michigan; and Edward R. Stettinius, Jr., who was the United States representative on the United Nations Security Council. They were not especially happy with their female colleague, dismissing her as an emotional, rattlebrained woman. Without her knowledge, these four gentlemen met and assigned Mrs. Roosevelt to Committee Three, which would deal with humanitarian, educational, and cultural questions. She imagined them saying, "Ah, here's the safe spot for her—Committee Three. She can't do much harm there!" She assumed that they wanted to keep her away from committees dealing with political and economic matters simply because she was a woman. "I kept my thoughts to myself and humbly agreed to serve where I was asked to serve," she wrote.

When the London session got under way, Eleanor Roosevelt quickly became known as the hardest-working and best-informed member of the American delegation. Nothing could make her miss a meeting. When King George and Queen Elizabeth invited her to Buckingham Palace for lunch, she accepted gracefully. But she told them that she would have to leave early to attend a subcommittee meeting.

To everyone's surprise, Committee Three, Mrs. Roosevelt's "safe spot," turned out to be a hotbed of controversy. The end of the war in Europe had left more than a million refugees stranded in displaced persons' camps. The Soviet Union insisted on forced repatriation—all displaced persons must be returned to their homelands. Yet many of the refugees from eastern Europe were opponents of the Communist regimes that were seizing power in their countries. They feared that forced repatriation would mean imprisonment or death. The United States and other Western nations supported the right of political asylum—allowing refugees to choose their own homes. The issue of refugee repatriation landed in the lap of Committee Three.

With the U.S. delegation at a meeting of the UN General Assembly, September 1947.

Since that was Mrs. Roosevelt's committee, it was up to her to speak for the United States. Her opponent in the General Assembly debate would be Andrei Vishinsky, the head of the Soviet delegation, one of Russia's great legal minds, and a powerful orator. "I was badly frightened," Eleanor recalled. "I trembled at the thought of speaking against the famous Mr. Vishinsky."

As she had done so many times before at lectures and press conferences, Mrs. Roosevelt spoke without notes when she addressed the delegates of the UN's original fifty-one member nations. Afterward Andrei Vishinsky delivered a fiery speech that lasted late into the night. Finally the General Assembly voted against forced repatriation. The refugees were free to choose their own homes.

The vote was a political triumph for the United States and a personal victory for Eleanor Roosevelt. The tall lady in the flowered hat had emerged as the world's foremost spokesperson for human rights. Her fellow American delegates, who had opposed her appointment, now had to eat their words. As Senator Vandenberg put it: "I want to say that I take back everything I ever said about her, and believe me it's been plenty."

Mrs. Roosevelt had helped determine the fate of thousands of displaced persons, yet she had never seen a refugee camp. When her fellow delegates returned home at the end of the UN session, she flew to Germany on an Air Force plane and visited several camps. One of them was Zilcheim, where Jewish survivors of Nazi death camps had built a stone monument inscribed "To the Memory of All Jews Who Died in Germany."

As she toured the camp, a ragged boy about twelve years old approached with his little brother, who was about six. He did not know his own name, where his home was, or what had happened to his parents. He wanted to sing for her, he said, so Eleanor and her guides stopped to listen. Standing in the mud, gripping his brother's hand, the youngster lifted his head and sang "A Song of Freedom."

Mrs. Roosevelt served as a UN delegate throughout Truman's two terms as president. During those years of Cold War suspicion and hostility, she held firm to her belief that a strong United Nations was the best hope for a lasting peace.

Lending a sympathetic ear to a refugee woman in Germany.

In 1946, she was elected chair of the United Nations' eighteen-member Human Rights Commission, which had been instructed to draft an international bill of rights. The commission's task was to define the basic rights of people all over the world, such as the right to free speech and a fair trial, or the right to an education and a decent standard of living. During the next two years Mrs. Roosevelt proved herself a skillful diplomat as she mediated among the clashing views of delegates from different nations and cultures, each with its own ideas about the meaning of "human rights."

When the commission fell behind in its work, she drove her colleagues mercilessly, insisting on fourteen- and sixteen-hour days. The delegate from Panama begged Mrs. Roosevelt to remember that UN delegates have human rights, too. She replied that their sessions would be shorter if their speeches weren't so long-winded.

On December 10, 1948, at three A.M., the Universal Declaration of Human Rights finally came to a vote and was overwhelmingly approved by the United Nations General Assembly. Then something happened that never happened at the UN before or since. The delegates rose to give a standing ovation to a single delegate—a moving tribute to Eleanor Roosevelt's leadership.

Expressed as Mrs. Roosevelt wanted, in simple and eloquent prose, the Universal Declaration has now been published in the native languages of all countries. To this day, it stands as the most widely recognized statement of the rights to which every person on this planet is entitled.

During her years as a United Nations delegate, Eleanor Roosevelt continued to lecture, broadcast, and write. Her daily newspaper column was as popular as ever, she contributed to magazines, and she worked on the second and third volumes of her autobiography. In constant demand as a speaker, she delivered more than one hundred lectures a year, broadcast a daily radio commentary, and hosted a weekly television interview show, one of the first of its kind. *Variety*, the entertainment industry weekly, said that her radio talks ranked among the "finest pieces of speaking ever done by a woman on the air."

Her crowning
achievement at the
United Nations.
She called the Dec-
laration a "magna
carta for mankind."

A television
appearance.

"As time went on, the fact that I kept myself well occupied made my loneliness less acute," she wrote. "My philosophy has been that if you have work to do and do it to the best of your ability you will not have much time to think about yourself."

Her continuing popularity with the American people astonished politicians in both parties and infuriated anti-Roosevelt columnists. In a 1948 poll conducted by the *Woman's Home Companion,* Mrs. Roosevelt placed first among the nation's ten most popular personalities, ahead of President Truman and generals Douglas MacArthur and Dwight D. Eisenhower. The annual Gallup Poll on the most admired women in the world regularly put Eleanor Roosevelt at the top of the list.

She was described in these years by Maureen Corr, a secretary hired to assist the ailing Malvina Thompson. "I expected some kind of royalty," Maureen said of her new boss, "and here was a warm, kind, embracing person. Her total simplicity was such a revelation to me, her lack of any feeling of self-importance."

Once, on a trip for the United Nations, Mrs. Roosevelt's companion leaned over and touched her arm as their plane prepared to land. "Look!" he said, pointing to a huge crowd gathered at the airport. "That's not for us," she replied. "Someone important must be flying in." When they stepped off the plane, she discovered with genuine surprise that the crowd was waiting for her.

When she wasn't on the move, Eleanor divided her time between a small apartment on New York's Washington Square and her cottage at Hyde Park. During the depression, she had taken over the former furniture factory on Val-Kill Creek and transformed it into a rambling, two-story guest house for visiting relatives and friends. After Franklin's death, when the big house at Hyde Park was turned over to the government, Eleanor made the converted factory her own year-round home. Her old friends Marion Dickerman and Nancy Cook continued to live nearby, in the original stone cottage they had once shared with Eleanor. In 1948 she bought out their interest in the property, and Marion and Nan moved away. "I am afraid the many children we have with us in the summer were too much for their peace and quiet," Eleanor remarked.

By then, Val-Kill had become the lively center of Eleanor's family and personal life. Her son Elliott and his family had moved into a cottage that FDR had built for himself on a bluff above Eleanor's place. Later, John and his family occupied the stone cottage vacated by Marion and Nan. At Eleanor's cottage, the guest rooms were usually filled. Grandchildren scampered in and out of the house, often in dripping swimming suits. Visiting dignitaries and old associates from the New Deal days sat around the fireplace in the living room, debating and reminiscing late into the night. At Thanksgiving and Christmas, family and friends gathered around a dining room table stretched to its limits as Eleanor presided, serving the food herself from a side table.

Isabella Halsted, Anna Roosevelt's stepdaughter, never forgot the Thanksgiving dinner she attended as a young girl. Before dinner, Eleanor made it a point to seek out and chat personally with each child there. At the end of the festive midday meal, after dessert had been served, she rose from her place at the head of the table, apologized to everyone, and

Eleanor ties a ribbon for her granddaughter Sally, John Roosevelt's daughter.

excused herself. She had to go upstairs to finish packing, she explained. She was flying off to India that evening.

Eleanor's bedroom at Val-Kill overlooked a pond in which sunrise and sunset were reflected. During the summer months she spent her nights on a sleeping porch surrounded by trees, where she was lulled to sleep by a chorus of frogs and awakened by singing birds. She arose early, flipped over her mattress, made her bed, and started the day with a brisk walk through the woods, accompanied by Franklin's Scotty dog, Fala. "Fala accepted me after my husband's death," she wrote, "but I was just someone to put up with until the master should return."

Eleanor felt that those closest to her—her family and intimate friends—were far more important than any of her activities as an influential world figure. Some of her old friends were still close by. Joe and Trude Lash spent

A walk with Fala at Val-Kill.

a great deal of time with Eleanor both at Val-Kill and in New York City. Lorena Hickok had moved to a small apartment in Hyde Park village and was usually the first person Eleanor called when she went up to Val-Kill. Hick helped gather research material for some of Eleanor's articles and books, and in 1954, the two women collaborated on a book titled *Ladies of Courage.*

When Eleanor traveled, she arranged her schedule so that during the year she could see not only her children and grandchildren, who were scattered around the country, but also Esther Lape in Connecticut, Earl Miller in Florida, and others close to her. When she couldn't visit, she never failed to send cards and gifts on special occasions. "No relationship was ever terminated because of her neglect or thoughtlessness," Joseph Lash observed. "If the other person was forgetful, she was careful, in reminding him, not to make him feel guilty."

The newest member of her charmed circle of close friends was a handsome young physician named David Gurewitsch. They met in 1947 on a flight to Geneva. "The people I love mean more to me than all the public things," she told him. "I only do the public things because there are a few close people whom I love dearly & who matter to me above everything else. There are not so many of them & you are now one of them and I shall just have to try not to bother you too much!"

David became Eleanor's frequent companion for dinner and the theater, and for long walks at Val-Kill. When he married, Eleanor befriended his wife, Edna. Eventually the three of them joined in buying a townhouse in New York City that they converted into two separate apartments. There was little Eleanor did that was not shared with David and Edna.

For all the comforts of home and the warm pleasures of family and friendship, Eleanor Roosevelt continued to drive herself without letup. She never took a real vacation. Some of her friends worried that her hectic work schedule masked underlying feelings of melancholy. "For the first time I feel she is driven by some inner compulsion that will never let her come to rest," remarked an adviser at the UN.

Certainly there were times when Eleanor felt weary and depressed, when she withdrew silently into herself. She worried especially about her children, about their stormy marriages and uncertain careers. Their troubles seemed to be endless and weighed heavily on her heart. "All of us made life hard for her," Elliott wrote later. "All of us failed her."

And while she had loving and loyal friends, trusted confidants to whom she could pour out her heart, loneliness was her companion, too. She once wrote that Franklin's death had left a "big vacuum which nothing, not even the passage of years, would fill."

Loving others and losing herself in work were remedies for loneliness. And yet Eleanor Roosevelt worked hard because she had the energy and will to do so, and because she thoroughly enjoyed the tasks she set for herself. She had always found a sense of fulfillment in being useful. And

At a village near Delhi, India, 1952.

now more than ever, she had the sweet satisfaction of fighting for causes she believed in and knowing that she was leaving her mark on the affairs of the world.

During her years alone, Eleanor Roosevelt continued to be an influential figure in the Democratic Party. She spoke out forcefully on civil rights, nuclear disarmament, and other issues that mattered to her. Meanwhile, she traveled to virtually every corner of the globe, first as a goodwill ambassador from the State Department, and later as a private citizen.

On her trip to India in 1952, when she was sixty-seven, she was greeted at the airport by Prime Minister Jawaharlal Nehru and his sister, Mme. Pandit, who placed a garland of cloves and fragrant beads around her neck. "I have come here to learn," Mrs. Roosevelt said. During her thirty-day tour she addressed the Indian parliament, dined with maharajahs, rode through packed city streets and dusty village roads, crept into native mud huts, placed a wreath at Mahatma Gandhi's tomb, and saw the Taj Mahal in moonlight.

In the city of Allahabad, where she received an honorary university degree, she offered to meet with a delegation of students who had signed an open letter protesting her visit and denouncing "American imperialism." During the meeting, thousands of other students, shouting and chanting, gathered outside the high fence surrounding the Nehru family compound where Mrs. Roosevelt was staying. Nehru's sister, Mme. Pandit, tried to calm the angry students. When she failed, Eleanor asked to speak to them herself.

Going outside, she climbed up on a chair perched on top of a table, so the students on the other side of the fence could see her. They demanded that she leave the compound and meet with them in the university auditorium. She agreed. And she insisted on going alone, despite the anxious objections of the Nehru family and university officials.

At the jammed auditorium, Mrs. Roosevelt spoke briefly. Then she answered questions about American policies toward India and the rest of the Third World. Though not willing to accept all of her answers, the students left the meeting with admiration for the courage of their visitor and her disarming goodwill.

Back home, during the presidential campaign of 1952, Eleanor supported Democrat Adlai Stevenson. When General Dwight D. Eisenhower, a Republican, won the election, he decided not to reappoint Mrs. Roosevelt to her post at the United Nations. She had once told reporters that she wanted to devote the rest of her active life to the UN. As good as her word, she volunteered to work with the American Association for the United Nations (AAUN), a citizen's group that was attempting to gain support for the UN among the American people.

Shortly after Eisenhower's inauguration, Mrs. Roosevelt moved into a small, sparsely furnished cubicle at the AAUN's New York headquarters, insisting that it would suffice as her new office. "She walked into it as if it were the Gold Room at the White House," wrote a reporter, "and after a moment it did seem quite grand."

Freed of her official duties at the United Nations, she now traveled more widely than ever. For several years, she circled the globe almost yearly. During the 1950s, she made two trips to Japan and three to Israel. She journeyed through Europe and South America, visited Indonesia, the Philippines, Thailand, Iran, Turkey, and Morocco, and met with women's groups, students, high officials, and ordinary citizens at every stop.

"No, I have not slackened my pace," she told a reporter on the eve of her seventieth birthday in 1954. "At least, not yet. I probably shall. Everybody does."

The AAUN celebrated her birthday with a festive fund-raising dinner at New York's Waldorf Astoria Hotel. More than a thousand guests attended, including UN Secretary-General Dag Hammarskjöld, his predecessor, Trygve Lie, and Mrs. Roosevelt's arch opponent at the UN, Andrei Vishinsky. The Soviet delegate showed up unexpectedly, explaining that he wanted to pay tribute to a gallant lady. He would be "very glad to sit anywhere," he said.

Eleanor's family was there too, and, as she concluded her remarks, she paid her own tribute to them. "As for accomplishments, I just did what I had to do as things came along," she said. "I got the most satisfaction from my work at the UN." And yet more than achievements, she continued, "I treasure the love of my children, the respect of my children, and I would

In Israel, talking with Arab Sheik Suleiman Ali en Sayid and Israeli Colonel Michael Haneghi, 1952.

Visiting a farm in Japan, 1953.

Eleanor cuts her 70th-birthday cake.

never want my children or grandchildren to feel that I had failed them."

At the age of seventy her hair was gray and her tall figure had thickened, but she continued to follow a rigorous schedule. Up early, she did her morning sit-ups "to get the kinks out," took her long walk if time allowed, and launched into the day's activities. She now had twenty-three grandchildren and great-grandchildren to entertain at Val-Kill. "Life has got to be lived—that's all there is to it," she said.

"OF COURSE I KNOW — IT'S MRS. ROOSEVELT"

Cartoonist Herbert Block (Herblock) contributed this drawing to the AAUN in celebration of Mrs. Roosevelt's 70th birthday.

She had long wanted to visit the Soviet Union. In 1957, at the age of seventy-three, she finally had a chance to make the trip as a correspondent for the New York *Post*. She traveled from Moscow and Leningrad to far-away Tashkent and Samarkand, trying "to understand what was happening in Russia by looking at the country through Russian eyes."

Before going home, she was invited to visit Soviet Premier Nikita S. Khrushchev at his vacation villa in Yalta on the Black Sea. They sat on his porch for three hours and debated just about every issue that had been raised during the Cold War. Afterward, Khrushchev's family joined them for refreshments.

"Can I tell our papers that we had a friendly conversation?" Khrushchev asked.

"You can say that we had a friendly conversation but that we differ," Eleanor replied.

Khrushchev grinned broadly. "Well, at least we didn't shoot at each other!" he exclaimed.

With David and Edna Gurewitsch in Leningrad (now St. Petersburg), Russia.

"There is so much to do. . . ."

"For some time my children and my friends have been warning me that I must slow down," said Eleanor Roosevelt. "I am willing to slow down but I just don't know how."

She was slowing down a little. "My Day" now appeared only three days a week. However, she continued with her monthly magazine column and a variety of books and articles, with her work for the AAUN, and with the lectures that still took her all over the country. At seventy-five she returned to teaching, as a visiting lecturer at Brandeis University. And she began a new television series called *The Prospects of Mankind* and invited

Dr. Martin Luther King to be her first guest. Sixteen years after her husband's death, she was still America's "Most Admired Woman."

When John F. Kennedy became president in 1961, Eleanor Roosevelt took on several assignments for him. Once again she became a delegate to the United Nations. She accepted an appointment to the Advisory Council of the Peace Corps. And she agreed to chair President Kennedy's Commission on the Status of Women. "There is so much to do," she said, "so many engrossing challenges, so many heartbreaking and pressing needs, so much in every day that is profoundly interesting. But, I suppose I must slow down."

It did not seem possible that she would ever slow down, but age was catching up with her at last. For the first time in her life, her energy flagged and she had to cancel appointments. She tried to dismiss her aches and pains, telling a friend, "If you pay too much attention to them, the first thing you know you're an invalid."

Eleanor struggled to remain active until the summer of 1962, when doctors insisted that she enter the hospital for extensive tests. After she was discharged, she felt better for a while. She was able to visit Campobello Island for the dedication of the Franklin Delano Roosevelt Memorial Bridge, linking the Canadian island to the United States mainland. On the way home, she stopped for a visit with Esther Lape, one of her oldest friends. "I am on the way to recovery," she said.

She was working on her last book, *Tomorrow Is Now,* when illness forced her to return to the hospital. Her doctors knew now that she was suffering from a complicated and untreatable blood disease. For her seventy-eighth birthday, she gave orders from her hospital bed that she wanted a party at the New York townhouse she shared with David and Edna Gurewitsch—a party for little children. On October 11, a few friends with their children and grandchildren gathered there for ice cream, favors, and a birthday cake with a single glowing candle.

A week later, Eleanor was sent home. She told David that she did not wish to linger as a helpless invalid. Lying weakly in bed, drifting in and out of consciousness, she must have recalled so many scenes, so many moments from the past. *"You are not afraid are you?"* asked her father, looking down at her from his horse. And he swept her up and held her high in the air and kissed her.

"She was not afraid of death at all," wrote Trude Lash. "She was so weary and so infinitely exhausted. . . ."

She died on November 7, 1962, after a severe stroke.

"Our dear Mrs. Roosevelt died last evening . . . ," wrote Edna Gurewitsch. "Around a quarter of nine, I saw from my bedroom window, the simple casket leaving the house, it being placed in the hearse and Mrs. Roosevelt alone with David driving away from 74th Street for the last time. I called out many goodbyes from the window."

One woman called *The New York Times* to verify the time of Mrs. Roosevelt's death. "But she couldn't have died at 6:15," the woman sobbed. "We were eating dinner then and we were happy."

Eleanor Roosevelt was buried next to her husband in the rose garden at Hyde Park, as President Kennedy and two former presidents, Eisenhower and Truman, watched. Lyndon Johnson, who would become president in

A president, two former presidents, and a future president attended Eleanor Roosevelt's funeral in the rose garden at Hyde Park. To the right of the cross are President John F. Kennedy, Vice-President Lyndon B. Johnson, and former presidents Harry S. Truman and Dwight D. Eisenhower. To the left of the cross are Franklin D. Roosevelt, Jr., and Mrs. John F. Kennedy.

a year's time, stood nearby. After the service, David Gurewitsch went up
to General Eisenhower and asked, "How could it happen that you did not
make use of this lady? We had no better ambassador." Eisenhower
shrugged and moved away.

"I made use of her," said Truman, who had overheard. "I told her she
was the First Lady of the World."

Toward the end of her life, as she looked back "along the way I had come,
trying to get a long-range view of the journey I had made," Eleanor
Roosevelt recalled some of the battles she had fought, both public and
private, and the victories she had won.

"It was not until I reached middle age that I had the courage to develop
interests of my own . . ." she wrote. "From that time on, though I have
had many problems, though I have known the grief and loneliness that are
the lot of most human beings . . . I have never been bored, never found
the days long enough for the range of activities with which I wanted to fill
them. And, having learned to stare down fear, I long ago reached the
point where there is no living person whom I fear, and few challenges that
I am not willing to face."

Eleanor Roosevelt
Photo Album

With her father at their Long Island country house.

In Venice on her honeymoon. Franklin snapped the photo.

Expecting their first child.

Sailing with friends at Campobello.

With Sara and Anna on her pony, "Daisy."

Eleanor and her five children.

A picnic with Nancy Cook, Peggy Levenson, Marion Dickerman, and John.

*Eleanor and Malvina
Thompson visit Elizabeth
Read in Connecticut.*

*Seeing Franklin, Jr.,
off to Europe.*

Campaigning in Warm
Springs, Georgia.

With Malvina Thompson
and Earl Miller at Val-Kill.

Voting at Hyde Park.

*Arriving in London,
she is met by
King George and
Queen Elizabeth.*

*Aboard an aircraft
carrier in the South
Pacific.*

On Guadalcanal beside a downed Japanese Zero.

Putting Fala through his paces.

Sightseeing in Japan.

At a camp for Jewish children from Morocco.

With President John F. Kennedy in 1961.

Eleanor with the Heart Fund child.

At Campobello with Maureen Corr.

Mrs. Roosevelt waves goodbye
from a train window.

A Visit to Val-Kill

"The greatest thing I have learned is how good it is to come home again," Eleanor Roosevelt once told a friend. Mrs. Roosevelt lived in many places, but her one true home was her beloved Val-Kill Cottage at Hyde Park, where she spent much of her time during the last quarter-century of her life.

Today Val-Kill is the only national historic site dedicated to the memory of a First Lady. Visitors approach along a bumpy lane that passes through fields and woods, winds around a pond, crosses a noisy plank bridge, and ends in a grove of pines. The site has two main buildings: the original stone cottage built in 1925 that Eleanor shared with Nancy Cook and Marion Dickerman; and behind it, half-hidden among the trees, the rambling, gray-stucco structure built in 1926 to house Val-Kill Industries, the experimental furniture factory started by Eleanor and her friends.

When the factory closed during the Great Depression, it was converted into apartments for Mrs. Roosevelt and her secretary Malvina Thompson, with several guest rooms to handle the overflow from the big house at Hyde Park. After Franklin Roosevelt's death in 1945, Eleanor turned the big house over to the U.S. government and adopted the converted factory, renamed Val-Kill Cottage, as her permanent home. Though she

Val-Kill Cottage.

maintained a New York apartment, the cottage was the center of her personal life—a gathering place for family and friends, a mecca for visiting dignitaries, and a sanctuary where she could relax or work uninterrupted late into the night.

Preserved much as Mrs. Roosevelt left it, Val-Kill Cottage is now a museum exhibiting her belongings and furnishings. The original Stone Cottage houses the headquarters of the Eleanor Roosevelt Center at Val-Kill, and, if not in other use, is also open to the public. A tour of the grounds includes the flower garden, the swimming pool, and Val-Kill Pond. Visitors are invited to view a film about Eleanor Roosevelt in the playhouse adjacent to Val-Kill Cottage.

About two miles west, the Franklin D. Roosevelt Home, Library, and Museum displays many mementoes of Eleanor Roosevelt's life and career. Mrs. Roosevelt is buried next to her husband in the mansion's rose garden.

Eleanor Roosevelt National Historic Site, Route 9G, Hyde Park, N.Y. Open seven days a week from May through October. The site is closed from Thanksgiving Day through the last day of February. The rest of the year it is open on Saturday and Sunday only.

Home of Franklin D. Roosevelt National Historic Site, Route 9, Hyde Park, N.Y. Next to the historic site is the *Franklin D. Roosevelt Library and Museum*. Open 9 A.M. to 5 P.M. every day except Thanksgiving, Christmas, and New Year's Day.

For further information contact the Superintendent, Roosevelt-Vanderbilt National Historic Sites, 249 Albany Post Road, Hyde Park, N.Y. 12538. Telephone (914) 229-9115.

Eleanor's living room. She sat in the wing chair behind the table.

Eleanor and Helen Keller in conversation.

Books About and by Eleanor Roosevelt

Eleanor Roosevelt's friend and biographer Joseph P. Lash was the first author to make use of the massive Eleanor Roosevelt manuscript collection at the Franklin D. Roosevelt Library in Hyde Park. Lash wrote two volumes of definitive biography: *Eleanor and Franklin: The Story of Their Relationship Based on Eleanor Roosevelt's Private Papers* (New York: W.W. Norton, 1971), and *Eleanor: The Years Alone* (New York: W.W. Norton, 1972). Two additional volumes of personal letters, edited with commentary by Lash, offer revealing insights into Eleanor Roosevelt's private life: *Love, Eleanor: Eleanor Roosevelt and Her Friends* (Garden City, N.Y.: Doubleday, 1982), and *A World of Love: Eleanor Roosevelt and Her Friends, 1943–1962* (Garden City, N.Y.: Doubleday, 1984). Also by Lash are *Eleanor Roosevelt: A Friend's Memoir* (Garden City, N.Y.: Doubleday, 1964), and *Life Was Meant To Be Lived: A Centenary Portrait of Eleanor Roosevelt* (New York: W.W. Norton, 1984). Lash's encyclopedic yet sensitive body of work is indispensable to any serious student of Eleanor Roosevelt's life and career.

Another major work based on primary sources, including some recently opened materials not available to Lash, is Blanche Wiesen Cook's controversial and frankly speculative biography, *Eleanor Roosevelt: Volume*

One, 1884–1933 (New York: Viking, 1992). This spirited new interpretation focuses on Eleanor's personal relationships and her emergence as a feminist and political activist.

A scholarly, insightful, and highly readable account of Eleanor and Franklin's courtship and marriage before the presidential years can be found in Geoffrey C. Ward's *Before the Trumpet: Young Franklin Roosevelt, 1882–1905* (New York: Harper & Row, 1985), and *A First-Class Temperament: The Emergence of Franklin Roosevelt* (New York: Harper & Row, 1989).

Two compact yet informative biographies are J. William T. Young's warmly admiring *Eleanor Roosevelt: A Personal and Public Life* (Boston: Little, Brown, 1985); and Lois Scharf's *Eleanor Roosevelt: First Lady of American Liberalism* (Boston: Twayne, 1987), which emphasizes the public figure and the political culture in which she moved and draws on recent scholarship in women's history.

Without Precedent: The Life and Career of Eleanor Roosevelt (Bloomington: Indiana University Press, 1984), a collection of scholarly essays edited by Joan Hoff-Wilson and Marjorie Lightman, explores the First Lady's political growth, her views on vital issues, and her political friendships.

Books about Eleanor Roosevelt's network of friends include Kenneth S. Davis's *Invincible Summer: An Intimate Portrait of the Roosevelts Based on the Recollections of Marion Dickerman* (New York: Atheneum, 1974), and Doris Faber's *The Life of Lorena Hickok: E.R.'s Friend* (New York: William Morrow, 1980). Lorena Hickok's own account of her friendship with Eleanor appears in *Eleanor Roosevelt: Reluctant First Lady* (New York: Dodd, Mead, 1962). *Mother and Daughter: The Letters of Eleanor and Anna Roosevelt*, edited by Bernard Asbell (New York: Coward, McCann, & Geoghegan, 1982), includes an extensive commentary by the editor.

Eleanor Roosevelt's own recollections provide an engaging and enlightening introduction to her life and thought. Though she exercises strict discretion and avoids certain personal topics, her memoirs are disarmingly candid and capture her extraordinary personality. They were published originally as *This Is My Story* (New York: Harper & Bros., 1937), *This I*

Remember (New York: Harper & Bros., 1949), and *On My Own* (New York: Harper & Bros., 1958). The three volumes are collected in an abridged one-volume edition which includes a new fourth section, "The Search for Understanding," and a preface by Mrs. Roosevelt: *The Autobiography of Eleanor Roosevelt* (New York: Harper & Row, 1961; Boston: G. K. Hall, 1984, with a new introduction by John Roosevelt Boettiger). Quotations from the memoirs come from this single volume.

Mrs. Roosevelt wrote many other books on a wide range of subjects. They include *It's Up to the Women* (New York: Frederick A. Stokes, 1933), *The Moral Basis of Democracy* (New York: Howell, Soskin, 1940), *India and the Awakening East* (New York: Harper & Bros., 1953), *You Learn By Living* (New York: Harper & Bros., 1960), and *Tomorrow Is Now* (New York: Harper & Row, 1963). A selection of the First Lady's newspaper columns appears in *Eleanor Roosevelt's My Day*, three volumes edited by Rochelle Chadakoff and David Elmblidge (New York: Pharos Books, 1989–1991). Transcriptions of Mrs. Roosevelt's press conferences are collected in *The White House Press Conferences of Eleanor Roosevelt*, edited by Maurine H. Beasley (New York: Garland Publications, 1983).

A listing of magazine articles by Eleanor Roosevelt, compiled by the Franklin D. Roosevelt Library, runs to thirty-three pages and ranges from "What I Want Most Out of Life" (*Success Magazine*, March 1927) to "What Has Happened to the American Dream?" (*The Atlantic*, April 1961). Along with its vast collection of letters, documents, and published works concerning Eleanor Roosevelt, the Roosevelt Library has scripts of her radio broadcasts, texts of speeches, transcriptions of interviews, oral histories, thousands of photographs, home movies, and miles of film footage.

Acknowledgments and Picture Credits

I am grateful to Isabella Halsted, Curtis Roosevelt, Richard Sachs, and Eleanor and Van Seagraves for sharing their recollections of Eleanor Roosevelt with me. My thanks also to Paul McLaughlin and the other staff members at the Franklin D. Roosevelt Library in Hyde Park, and to Darryl Vernado and Patrick O'Hara who guided me through the Eleanor Roosevelt National Historic Site at Val-Kill.

All photographs and other illustrations not specifically credited below were furnished by the Franklin D. Roosevelt Library and are herewith gratefully acknowledged:

The Bettmann Archive: frontispiece, x, 17, 31 (top), 35, 44, 59, 62, 67, 78, 96, 101, 103, 105, 111, 112, 120, 121, 124, 130, 145, 188

Russell Freedman: 186

Historical Picture Service: 99

Life Picture Services: 126

New York Times Pictures: 167

The Oakland Museum, Dorothea Lange Collection: 107

Press Information Bureau, Government of India: 158

Wide World Photos: 49 (right), 75, 85, 86, 94, 114, 141

Index

DATE DUE

JAN 2 2 2001			
FEB 0 5 2001			
MAY 2 3			

DEMCO